HOW TO START YOUR OWN
RELIGION

Form a Church, Gain Followers, Become Tax-Exempt, and

Sway the Minds of Millions in five Easy Steps

PHILIP ATHANS
Founder and Sole Member of the Church of Phil

Adamsmedia
Avon, Massachusetts

Published by
Adams Media, a division of F+W Media, Inc.
57 Littlefield Street, Avon, MA 02322. U.S.A.
www.adamsmedia.com

ISBN 10: 1-4405-3858-1
ISBN 13: 978-1-4405-3858-2
eISBN 10: 1-4405-3882-4
eISBN 13: 978-1-4405-3882-7

Printed in the United States of America.

10 9 8 7 6 5 4 3 2 1

Library of Congress Cataloging-in-Publication Data
is available from the publisher.

This publication is designed to provide accurate and authoritative information with regard to the subject matter covered. It is sold with the understanding that the publisher is not engaged in rendering legal, accounting, or other professional advice. If legal advice or other expert assistance is required, the services of a competent professional person should be sought.

—From a *Declaration of Principles* jointly adopted by a Committee of the American Bar Association and a Committee of Publishers and Associations

Many of the designations used by manufacturers and sellers to distinguish their product are claimed as trademarks. Where those designations appear in this book and Adams Media was aware of a trademark claim, the designations have been printed with initial capital letters.

This book is available at quantity discounts for bulk purchases.
For information, please call 1-800-289-0963.

CONTENTS

7   FOREWORD

11   INTRODUCTION. SO YOU WANT TO START YOUR OWN RELIGION

23   STEP 1. DOGMA: SO YOU HAVE SOMETHING TO SAY

25   CHAPTER 1. GOD IS . . . OR, THE GODS ARE . . .
      OR, THE POWERS THAT BE ARE . . .
      who and/or what is it you're worshiping in the first place?

33   CHAPTER 2. SO LET IT BE WRITTEN
      it's not a religion without some kind of holy text

43   CHAPTER 3. DELIVER THE MOST SACRED RITE
      give them something to eat, hold, walk around, step on, etc.

51   CHAPTER 4. WHAT DAY IS THIS?
      who says you can't have your own calendar?

57   CHAPTER 5. NO ONE EXPECTS *YOUR* INQUISITION
      for those special moments when you just have to crack some skulls

63   CHAPTER 6. SAMPLE RELIGION 1:
      SCHOLARS OF THE PARTICULARLY LONG BOOK
      they who don't get out much

69   STEP 2. CONVERTS: SO YOU DON'T GET LONELY

71   CHAPTER 7. SAVE THE FAITHFUL
      and keep them coming back for more

81   CHAPTER 8. GOD HELPS THOSE WHO HAVE
      CELEBRITY SPOKESPEOPLE
      who wouldn't believe a movie star?

87   CHAPTER 9. **UNLEASH THE FANATICS**
or rein them back in

91   CHAPTER 10. **MARCH OFF TO THE HOLY WARS**
at least threaten to, anyway, from time to time

95   CHAPTER 11. **SAMPLE RELIGION 2: THE CHURCH OF PHIL**
the gospel according to Me

99   STEP 3. **RITUAL: SO YOU HAVE SOMETHING TO DO**

101   CHAPTER 12. **ESTABLISH YOUR SHRINE, MEGA-CHURCH, FANE, OR OTHER TEMPLE**
because you have to meet somewhere

111   CHAPTER 13. **RELAX, IT'S A HOLY DAY**
or, work really hard, it's a holy day

119   CHAPTER 14. **BOOT YOUR SONS AND DAUGHTERS OUT OF THE NEST**
when it's time to grow up

125   CHAPTER 15. **I NOW PRONOUNCE YOU HUSBAND(S) AND/OR WIVE(S)**
and hurry, before they pass the defense of marriage act

133   CHAPTER 16. **CAST OUT THE FAITHLESS**
when only excommunication will do

139   CHAPTER 17. **ACCEPT BURNT OFFERINGS . . . OR NOT**
sometimes, you just have to sacrifice something . . . or someone

145   CHAPTER 18. **SAMPLE RELIGION 3: THE CULT OF THE BLUE ÖYSTER**
one hard rockin' evil biker death cult

149   STEP 4. **LIFE: SO YOU CAN INTERFERE WITH IT**

151   CHAPTER 19. **ABSTINENCE ONLY— UNLESS OTHERWISE INSTRUCTED**
sex is dirty and sinful, unless you're being fruitful and multiplying

157   CHAPTER 20. **EDUCATION: THE GREAT EVIL**
except if you attend one of our expensive private schools

165 **CHAPTER 21. THE LAW OF MAN**
but only if you can't qualify for tax-exempt status

169 **CHAPTER 22. THE LAW OF THE GODS**
cash, check, or major credit cards accepted

177 **CHAPTER 23. SAMPLE RELIGION 4:
SISTERHOOD OF THE PERPETUALLY PREGNANT**
birth control? we don't even know what that is

181 **STEP 5. DEATH: SO YOU CAN MAKE PEOPLE
MORE OR LESS AFRAID**

183 **CHAPTER 24. ASHES TO ASHES, DUST TO DUST**
saying goodbye to the dear departed

193 **CHAPTER 25. THE SWEET BYE AND BYE**
what to expect when you're expecting an afterlife

201 **CHAPTER 26. BACK AND BETTER THAN EVER**
rebirth and ascension, not necessarily in that order

213 **CHAPTER 27. SAMPLE RELIGION 5:
THE HOLY UNDERTAKERS OF GILTINÉ**
additional funeral parking in rear

217 **CONCLUSION. SO YOU'VE STARTED YOUR OWN RELIGION**
go with the gods, my friends, but be careful out there

219 **INDEX**

Acknowledgments

The idea for this book came to me from my former boss and current friend Peter Archer, but I will just have to learn to forgive him. He's actually a really nice guy.

Speaking of bosses, you would not believe me if I told you how much hard work editor Jennifer Lawler put into this thing, and how fast she brought it together. I hope her next author will be less cranky, and that she will learn not to reply to e-mails on Sunday. Nothing good ever comes of that.

And thank you to my mother, who was primarily responsible for my own religious upbringing (for not giving me one), and my father for making me go to the Greek Orthodox church only when my *papou* was visiting from Boston. Aside from a few key details they were the Mary and Joseph of the Church of Phil.

foreword

I suppose if you're reading this book you're at least wondering, "How hard is it to start a religion?" From my experience, the answer is, "Not very hard."

I would guess that religious leaders fall into three large groups: the true believers, the con artists, and the accidental leaders. True believers would not be reading this book, which pokes fun at something they feel is deadly serious. This is too bad, because they're probably the most in need of both structure *and* absurdity. But one of the major problems with true believers is that they're at the mercy of their ideas of what the god(s) want them to do. As one true believer said to me, "If God says it, then I will do it. If his commandment was that all men should wear pink tutus, I would be at my local ballet supply company looking for a size 38!" It's hard to argue with that kind of zeal. And it often leads to decisions that can kill off a religion. The Shakers are a good example. They were a celibate faith that also stopped taking new members in 1965. It's no surprise that as of 2010, the Shakers were down to their last three members.

The con men have it better. They look at their religions as a business. If it makes good tax sense to turn their burgeoning psychology cults into religious cults then that's the road they'll take. If it brings in more revenue to argue that being a renunciate and devoting all your time to the faith is *not* a more pious direction to go (thus keeping your followers employed), but that tithing 15 percent *is* a pious decision, then you'll have hard-working and well-tithing followers. The downside to being a con man is that con men are . . . well, con men. And that probably means they're at least a bit sociopathic and likely have problems with delayed gratification. They can get away with ostentatious wealth and violating all of their own commandments for a long time. But it usually comes back to bite them.

The last one is probably more common than you might guess. If you read about New Religious Movements (the PC term that has replaced "cults") as much as I do you might notice how often you come across this origin story: Someone started running an "encounter group," a "study group," or a "group therapy session," and suddenly realized they were actually leading a religious movement. It's not a difficult path to stumble down. A group of people who are focused intensely and being self-revealing to each other may find all types of mystical events or truths suddenly appear. They may hear the voice of God, paranormal phenomena (rapping sounds or objects moving) may begin to occur, members may begin to have insights into each other or into the world that seem supernatural. The group's bond grows tighter and they begin to believe that they have a message that needs to be given to the world or perhaps they have a truth that must be protected from the world. Suddenly, you have a full-blown new religion.

If you don't believe me about the ability of a group to produce paranormal phenomena, go research the Philip Experiment. In a nutshell, in the 1970s a group of people consciously decided to create a ghost. They were completely aware that this ghost was made up by the group and yet when contacted via séance the ghost performed as well or better than "real" ghosts supposedly contacted in other séances. Given that the ghost was fictional, the only explanation for the phenomena was the psychology of the group.

Why is it so easy to create a religion? Because humans need to order their world in the face of far too much information input and the awareness that there is far too much that lies on the other side of the walls of ignorance. H. P. Lovecraft (inspiration for numerous New Religious Movements) had it right when he wrote, "we live on a placid island of ignorance in the midst of black seas of infinity, and it was not meant that we should voyage far."

We will take any opportunity we can to find order and sense in our world. And if we can gather a group of people around us who will affirm our vision we will gladly grab hold with both hands. Evolution made us tribal creatures and that desire can easily be placated by a religious movement.

Unfortunately, that same tribal impulse tends to make us place one member of the group in the role of "leader" (priest, minister, guru, high-poobah). And that's where the trouble always begins. If you're reading this book you may be laughing about the idea of becoming the founder of a new religion—but don't laugh too hard. It's easier than you think, and laughing is no protection—go look up the Church of the SubGenius, Discordianism, or Thee Temple ov Psychick Youth. If you were to even casually move in that direction you could easily find yourself leading a small ragtag group of people who are looking to you for the next revelation, prophecy, ritual, or rule for living. This might lead to a fleet of Rolls Royces and your own island in the Fijis, but you better not disappoint your followers or they could viciously turn on you. On the other hand, do you really want to be responsible for someone else's life? Personally, I find running my own hard enough.

—Anthony Valterra, BA, Religious Studies; MA, Consciousness Studies; briefly an accidental religious leader

INTRODUCTION

So You Want to Start Your Own Religion

If you have ever observed the power, wealth, and privilege that accrue to leaders and practitioners of certain religions, you've probably thought, "You know, *I* should start my own religion. Then I would be the one who gets to decide if recreational drug use is an acceptable response to the crushing angst of adolescence." Or perhaps you have experienced a loftier sentiment and have toyed with the idea of creating a lasting ethos that will endure through the rest of human history, spreading enlightenment to the unenlightened for all time to come.

Either way, you've come to the right place. In *How to Start Your Own Religion*, you will discover the five steps you'll need to take to become the font of all that is good (or bad, depending). You'll learn everything you need to know to go about establishing a religion, gaining adherents, and running their lives. They will thank you for this by making offerings of money, time, sex, and food (and sex with food) unless you'd rather they didn't.

In Step 1, you will decide what kind of religion you wish to start. You will also create (or "receive from On High, in a dream") the religious texts that will dictate your religion's policies on questions such as one's right to control one's own body, one's obligation to share the wealth (e.g. "help the less fortunate"), and more.

In Step 2, you will find out how to spread the word and attract followers, converts, and fanatics, as well as what to do with them once you've got them.

In Step 3, you'll figure out where to gather for worship/adoration/ hanging out with your adherents, and work on all the little things that keep them coming back for more, including holy days, adulthood rites, and weddings—and learn how, when, and why to toss your unwelcome followers out.

In Step 4, you'll take it to the next level by insinuating yourself and your new faith into every last corner of your followers' lives, and have them thank you for it.

And finally, in Step 5, you'll develop ways to speed the dear departed off to wherever it is you think they're headed, and maybe bring a few of them back from the Great Beyond.

Getting Started

Establishing your own religion can be a daunting undertaking. So much to do and so much to decide! Let's start with a little survey, which will help you refine your thinking. Choose as many answers as you think are correct for each question, though your religion will be easier for followers to remember if you keep it to one answer per question. *Note*: Internal consistency is not required in any religion.

This is not a test, mind you. There are no right or wrong answers. It's all about opinion—oops, sorry, I mean *revelation!*

1. **How many gods are there?**
   A. None: Virtue is its own reward
   B. There can be only one
   C. 2–11
   D. 12 or more
   E. We're all gods
   F. Infinity

2. **Complete this sentence: God is . . . (or, the gods are . . .) (or the Powers That Be are . . .)**
   A. Love
   B. The all-powerful Creator(s) of the Universe
   C. Pretty much ambivalent about us
   D. Pissing me off
   E. Vengeful, wrathful, and other synonyms for angry
   F. Dead

3. **Our holy writing is contained in . . .**
   A. The eternal spirits of the faithful
   B. An epic poem of enduring beauty and grace
   C. An epic poem that's actually kind of over-long and a little boring
   D. This one book, which is the only book you'll ever need
   E. Beatles' records, played backward
   F. The steaming, bloody entrails of infidels

4. **The most important religious principle is ...**

   A. Be excellent to each other.

   B. Thou shalt not kill.

   C. In the case of the tax imposed by Chapter 21 (relating to tax on self-employment income) and the tax imposed by section 3101 (relating to tax on employees under the Federal Insurance Contributions Act)

   (1) If an amount is erroneously treated as self-employment income, or if an amount is erroneously treated as wages, and

   (2) If the correction of the error would require an assessment of one such tax and the refund or credit of the other tax, and

   (3) If at any time the correction of the error is authorized as to one such tax but is prevented as to the other tax by any law or rule of law (other than section 7122, relating to compromises), then, if the correction authorized is made, the amount of the assessment, or the amount of the credit or refund, as the case may be, authorized as to the one tax shall be reduced by the amount of the credit or refund, or the amount of the assessment, as the case may be, which would be required with respect to such other tax for the correction of the error if such credit or refund, or such assessment, of such other tax were not prevented by any law or rule of law (other than section 7122).

   D. Speed Limit 55

   E. Don't do the crime if you can't do the time.

   F. Rules are made to be broken.

5. **Our most sacred rite consists of . . .**
   A. This really pretty flower I picked this morning
   B. Twinkies
   C. Complex tea rituals that take so long to complete the first one isn't over yet
   D. A nice, lean piece of veal. Who doesn't love a nice, lean piece of veal?
   E. Blood. And I don't mean figuratively.
   F. I can only tell you if you sign this release first.

6. **What year is it?**
   A. Does anybody really know what time it is? Does anybody really care?
   B. 2012
   C. 4,256,321,031
   D. 0
   E. 1
   F. However many years it's been since I was born

7. **The chief weapon of your Inquisition is . . .**
   A. Surprise
   B. Fear
   C. Ruthless efficiency
   D. An almost fanatical devotion to the Pope
   E. Nice red uniforms
   F. All of the above

8. **What do you have to offer the faithful that no other religion does?**
   A. Enlightenment
   B. Eternal life
   C. Contentment
   D. Revenge
   E. Sex
   F. All of the above

9. **Your ideal celebrity spokesperson is . . .**
   A. No one
   B. Yourself
   C. Tom Cruise
   D. Oprah
   E. Stephen Baldwin
   F. That dog from the flea medicine commercial who's been sending you subliminal messages for months

10. **Fanatics are . . .**
    A. Dangerously imbalanced
    B. Fine if they switch to decaf
    C. To be used only in emergencies
    D. People you occasionally have to publicly disavow
    E. Your core audience
    F. The invincible army of righteousness

11. **When is the best time to fight a holy war?**
    A. Never
    B. If you're absolutely sure you can win
    C. Before all that sarin gas you bought from that North Korean guy expires
    D. After the thirteenth solstice before the end of the Great Migration of Givornius
    E. When someone steps to you
    F. Wait, who says you can *stop* fighting a holy war?

12. **Where do you plan to hold your sacred rites and ceremonies?**
    A. The whole world is our shrine
    B. Usually in the living room, but lately it's been kinda spilling over into the kitchen
    C. We rent the middle school gym, except during basketball season
    D. A sweet little temple on a hill
    E. A massive cathedral with flying buttresses and other architectural elements that sound vaguely dirty
    F. A stepped pyramid decorated with the blood of sacrificial virgins, and kick-ass Metallica posters

13. **Holy days are best observed . . .**
    A. In the loving company of family and friends
    B. Anywhere but at work
    C. With a massive feast
    D. By fasting
    E. With a lot of chanting, moaning, and candles
    F. Naked

14. **A boy becomes a man when he . . .**
    A. Accepts responsibility to lead a good, honest, nurturing, and loving life
    B. Turns eighteen
    C. Comes back from his pilgrimage or missionary trip
    D. Shotguns this beer
    E. Doesn't puke after shotgunning this beer
    F. Shoots this beer with a shotgun

15. **A girl becomes a woman when she . . .**
    A. Accepts responsibility to lead a good, honest, nurturing, and loving life
    B. Turns eighteen
    C. Has her first period
    D. Unfriends her parents on Facebook
    E. Texts a naked photo of herself to her fifteen-year-old boyfriend whom she is going to love forever and ever and ever
    F. Steals her BFF's boyfriend

16. **Marriage is . . .**
    A. A loving union between two or more consenting adults
    B. A loving union between a man and a woman
    C. A loving union between a man and several women
    D. A loving union between a woman and several men
    E. A loving union between me and all of the men/women in the church
    F. Banned

17. **Someone must be immediately excommunicated if he or she . . .**
    A. Harshes the group's mellow
    B. Commits a mortal sin, like listening to Marilyn Manson (or *not* listening to Marilyn Manson)
    C. Fails to adequately tithe
    D. Won't have sex with me
    E. Refuses to eat of the flesh of the unworthy
    F. Farts during the Holiest of Holy Ceremonies

18. **We sacrifice . . .**
    A. Nothing, the gods make no material demands on us
    B. Little pieces of paper on which we've written our sins
    C. Broken household items
    D. Anything that'll burn
    E. Stray pets
    F. I refuse to answer in accordance with my rights under the Fifth Amendment as such answer may tend to incriminate me

19. **Sex is to be enjoyed . . .**
    A. Between loving, consenting adults
    B. Between an adult man and an adult woman who love each other, or have had one too many appletinis
    C. Within the confines of marriage
    D. In some extremely specific way
    E. During the monthly Fornication Rite
    F. Constantly

20. **Children should be educated . . .**
   A. By their parents, in an all-vegan, bully-free home school environment
   B. In public schools, where they can learn to defend their faith against challenges
   C. In private, church-run schools, where they can be successfully indoctrinated
   D. In public schools compelled to teach our religion to all kids
   E. In the school of hard knocks
   F. Never

21. **The government is . . .**
   A. An antiquated, patriarchal, establishmentarian dinosaur
   B. Separate from my church
   C. An easy target for infiltration
   D. An impediment to the Truth
   E. Fine, so long as I can still be tax-free
   F. Awesome

22. **God (or the gods) expect(s) me to . . .**
   A. Live a life of love, peace, and harmony with all his/her/their creatures
   B. Seek enlightenment
   C. Pray regularly
   D. Pay regularly
   E. Rock
   F. Blow up stuff and kill people in his/her/their name(s)

23. **Dead bodies should be . . .**
    A. Disposed of with respect and dignity, according to the wishes of the departed
    B. Buried
    C. Cremated
    D. Left on a rock to be picked apart by scavengers
    E. Laid in a longboat which is then set afire and cast out to sea
    F. Eaten

24. **When you die, you . . .**
    A. Become one with the universe or, like, the Force or something
    B. Achieve enlightenment on a higher plane of existence
    C. Are reincarnated into the body of a human baby
    D. Are reincarnated into an animal or something, but hopefully not a bug—a tiger or, like, a great white shark would be awesome
    E. Go to Heaven/Next World/Arcadia If You've Led a Good Life, or Hell/Scary Bad Place/Underworld If You're a Sinner
    F. Rise up as an undead avenger to kick the ass of all who wronged you in life and eat their livers in front of their screaming faces

25. **After death, the truly holy will . . .**
    A. Get a second chance to lead a better life
    B. Guide loved ones from the Great Beyond
    C. Become an angel
    D. Become a ghost
    E. Become a demigod
    F. Become a new, way more badass god

If you chose mostly As, you might not be prepared to start your own religion, and would probably be cool just hanging around the Zen Center. If you chose a mixture of B, C, and D you should end up with something most people will at least recognize as a religion, and you'll have a lot of positive examples from which to draw inspiration. But if you ended up with a lot of Es and Fs, you might want to think about retaining counsel now.

However you came out, keep your answers in mind as you read the rest of this book. You'll find all sorts of handy tips and tricks to make all your goals come true. And you might just want to come back and change a few of your answers. That's okay; just make sure they're locked in before you start engraving those stone tablets. Stone is a very unforgiving medium. And don't forget to destroy any earlier drafts—you don't want your own version of the Dead Sea Scrolls bouncing around out there.

Dogma: So You Have Something to Say

The word "dogma" describes all the fun facts, fables, commandments, rituals, and truths you will expect your followers to study, learn, remember, and follow ... blindly, if possible.

CHAPTER 1

God Is ... or, the Gods Are ... or, the Powers That Be Are ...

who and/or what is it you're worshiping in the first place?

If you want to start your own religion, you're going to have to begin with some kind of deity, that is, a supreme being (or beings) in Charge of It All. Your followers will require some number of gods, goddesses, and/or higher power(s) to follow (hence, "followers"). It is this deity they will get pissed off at when life turns out the way it often does—better Him/Her/It/They than you. The various deities worshiped over the course of human history have very little in common except that all of them have an easily expressed identity and a clearly articulated mission statement. Your higher power's mission statement will become the rocky center of your entire religion.

Your Deity(ies)

Because this is the truly fundamental lynchpin of your entire religion, you'd better think carefully. Before you commit irrevocably to any decision, let's discuss a few options, beginning with the number of gods. This is crucial, as it sets the tone for your entire religion.

- If your religion recognizes no gods at all, your religion is considered to be *atheistic*, which means it's not actually a religion. You're now finished with this book. Go and enjoy a nice pulled-pork sandwich with cheese while you plan your wedding to your sister on the set of MSNBC, you godless heathen you.
- If your religion only recognizes one god (which is usually spelled with a capital "G") then your religion is *monotheistic*.
- If your religion recognizes a number of gods then you're *polytheistic*.
- If you think everything and everybody is a god, then your religion is *pantheistic*, and you have a very confusing eternity ahead of you.

Let's break these down:

There Is No "God" *Per Se*

If you start with the idea of atheism, what you're creating is a philosophy, not a religion. That's fine, but this isn't a book about creating your own philosophy. I'll be pitching that book next. Thank you for buying both of them.

There Can Be Only One

Monotheism is currently the most popular model (and was even before the release of the movie *Highlander*), adopted by some billions of Christians, Muslims, and Jews worldwide. Just as Christianity was born out of Judaism, and Islam developed from both Judaism and Christianity, it's perfectly fine to go ahead and adopt not just *a* god, but *the* God to head up your religion. Over the centuries, God has been reinterpreted in thousands of forms, by all sorts of splinter religions, sects, and cults, and try as some might, no one person has managed to speak exclusively for the same God claimed by all three of the major world religions. You are perfectly free to take a run at it yourself, or even form one of those splinter-sects of your own, an off-shoot of an existing religion.

You're also free to stretch your creative muscles and start with a completely fresh new god. You can call him anything you want, dress him up however you like, or even make Him a Her. Or a Goat.

More Than One, But Less Than Infinity

My mother used to say that if you have two of the same thing it's a collection. The same is true with gods. If you're looking to go down the polytheistic road, it's important to establish early on how many gods are actually running around out there. This collection of deities is called a *pantheon*. Though you only need two gods to call it a pantheon, you can stretch that number out literally to infinity, though that tends to send you into pantheistic territory, and we're not there yet. Let's call a pantheon some number of gods ranging from two to less than infinity.

Some cultures worship all sorts of gods, depending on what they're looking for help with at any given time, but a word of caution: There is such a thing as too much of a good thing. If you don't believe me, find one of your Catholic friends and give him two minutes (no Googling!) to name the Patron Saint of Convulsive Children. The correct answer is Saint Scholastica, and if he gets it right, well, that's one *devout* motherfucker.

Your religion is eventually going to have followers, and if no one can remember who they're supposed to be praying to when, it gets confusing and they'll end up at an easier religion. That's how people become Lutherans.

We're All Gods

Pantheism is religion's advanced-level game, and not for the novice. If everyone is a god, or worse, everyone is God, why would people come to your church and not expect you to come to theirs? Pretty soon everybody's going to each other's churches, getting distracted along the way having to pray to all those blades of grass, each of which is a god. Can't you feel the whole universe straining under the weight of it?

There are pros and cons to all of these approaches, and if you're particularly clever you can even find a way to make pantheism work for you. Having a lot of gods can get confusing, so a lot of religions have created clear hierarchies among the gods, and put greater focus on one god, who, like Zeus or Odin, fills a leadership role in the heavens. The rest of the gods can be organized much like a corporation's org chart, or a family tree, to make their relationships to each other, and to their worshipers, a little easier to track. For variety's sake, at least, I think polytheism is set for a comeback. It's been on the outs for a thousand years or so, and if there's one central truth to the universe it's that what goes around comes around.

Creating Your Pantheon

If you decide to choose more than one god, you'll need a cheat sheet for keeping track of all the gods and their foibles, which you will reveal to followers as you go along. Here's a handy spreadsheet to help you begin building a polytheistic pantheon, with a few examples to get you started.

BUILD-A-PANTHEON

NAME	GOD OF	RANK	LIKES	DISLIKES
Enlil	Air	Co-ruler	Storms and floods	People
Crom	Kicking ass	Divine hetman (chieftain)	Trouble	Pussies

NAME	GOD OF	RANK	LIKES	DISLIKES
Phil	This book	Senior regional manager	Ice cream	Cole Slaw

Number of Gods

Now it's time to make a commitment to the number of gods in your religion. This is quite simple. Just fill out the Statement of Commitment below.

Statement of Commitment:

"The number of gods in my religion is _____."

Excellent! Now, you need to define the nature of your god(s).

The Nature of God(s)

You may recall that this was one of the questions on the quiz in the Introduction. Before giving your final answer, however, take a few moments to consider whether you are choosing the appropriate nature of god(s) for your religion. Review these brief descriptions for further help.

God Is Love

I got that one from Oprah, and she should know. This is a nice way to start building a nice religion that will attract nice people to a nice god worshiped in a nice church on nice days with some nice cookies for everyone.

Keep that in mind when someone says something you don't like, though. If God is Love, it's hard to justify crashing airplanes into buildings in His Name. Likewise, you better be prepared with an answer for questions that begin, "If God is Love then why does He ... ?"— y'know— ... cause tsunamis, allow the Holocaust to happen, let that guy in the stands catch the ball that kept the Cubs out of the World Series. Stuff a truly Loving God wouldn't do.

God Is the All-powerful Creator of the Universe

This is what I like to call the Default God. This is God as a creative force, as a substitute for stuff like science, which is hard, so we need answers to questions like "How did we get here?" or "Why is the sky blue?" that are less confusing than the scientific answers and don't require math. The drawback to using this version of God is that everyone does it, so it's hard to stand out from the crowd.

The Gods Don't Care

If the deities don't give a shit about us either way, that explains earthquakes and the Bush Administration, but it can pose some challenges when it comes to recruiting followers. If you convince people that the all-powerful beings who run the universe don't care if they live or die, they tend to extend those beings the same courtesy.

God Is Pissing Me Off

This is a truly tough one, but might be worth a try. A religion based around protecting people from the gods, who are actively working against them, has a certain Old School appeal. And in this case "Old School" means *really* old ... like, *ancient*, literally. If the economy doesn't start getting better soon, we'll likely see religions of this type popping up all over the place. Get crackin' now and you could be ahead of the curve.

God Is Vengeful, Wrathful, and Other Synonyms for Angry

You might be surprised how many people you can attract to a religion based on trying to please a vengeful god(s) who wants to punish them. Your "God-fearing" types will line up for the Wrath of God(s), mostly because they think said wrath will be directed at other people while they watch from behind God(s)'s skirt, flipping off the damned and hurling "I Told You Sos" at them.

God Is Dead

This is another tricky one, but worth a try. Maybe your religion can be dedicated to bringing God back to life, if you imagine God to be someone you want to see again. On the other hand, you can set yourself up as leader of a protector cult that keeps a particularly nasty God from coming back to life. Fans of H. P. Lovecraft take note.

Nature of God(s)

Now it's time to make a commitment to the nature of God(s) in your religion. This is quite simple. Just fill out the Statement of Commitment below.

Statement of Commitment:

"The nature of God(s) in my religion is _____."

Congratulations! You are well on your way to starting your own religion. However, please do not put down this book just yet. The following chapters contain crucial information for starting your own religion. You know what they say: "Haste makes religions that don't stand up to rigorous intellectual investigation."

CHAPTER 2

So Let It Be Written

*it's not a religion without
some kind of holy text*

The Word of God (or gods, or Goddess, or Universal Consciousness) can come to you in any number of ways: burning bushes, rushing wind, a dream, on golden tablets in your hat, or on a pancake at the Waffle House. No one way of hearing from your chosen deity(ies) is better than another, but for some reason, people (e.g., potential followers) tend to be skeptical of someone who claims to have spoken with God directly. They prefer to believe in burning bushes, rushing winds, and so on.

If you've been contacted by God, gods, or etc., run through the story as it "really happened" with a few test converts. If they look at you like you're crazy, jot down on a slip of paper the moment you seemed to lose them and work on that bit until they buy it.

What Your Religion's Text Should Say

Writing down what God/gods/etc. say(s) is key to establishing a religion. No one believes in a religion that has no holy text. Your holy text can contain any or all of the following:

33

An Origin Story

How was the world, or even the entire universe, created? By God, or Goddess, or the gods, or someone or something, like the Titans, that came before the gods? The Bible starts with "In the beginning, God created the heavens and the earth," but yours could start with the origin of your religion, or the origin of you.

Reasons for Bad Things

Why do puppies have to die? Why were there Nazis? Why does ice cream make me fat? People turn to religion for help with questions like these. The world is a scary place and people need answers. If they can't find those answers in your holy writings, they'll move on to the next person's holy writings.

Reasons for Good Things

This is less in answer to people's questions than it is a supporting case for your religion. People enjoy things like love, babies, and money. If love comes from the union of the gods Boyus and Girlus, babies are formed in clay-flesh and placed in their mothers' wombs by Babus, and money is bestowed on those who pray to Coinus, and if you know how to get in touch with Boyus, Girlus, Babus, and Coinus, people will pay attention to you. Write this stuff down so you don't forget it.

The Difference Between Right and Wrong

Your writings can define this basic set of ethics, but be sure to include a statement of support for one or the other. People are looking for someone to tell them what to do and whether what they're doing is good or bad. Your holy text will help them sort it out.

Rules and Regulations

This covers, well . . . pretty much everything else in this book, actually.

Getting the Wording Right

The Word of God will help you justify all of the actions that you and your followers will take, so be careful to word things appropriately. You may wish to contact an attorney versed in contract law if you expect to saddle your followers with lots of financial obligations. A good editor can help you with the proper use of words such as "thou," "thee," and "shalt." That's not as easy as you think.

At the very least, have someone you trust read it through a couple of times, and ask him or her for notes. Even if that person says something like, "I don't buy this thing with the pony at all," it doesn't mean you need to lose the pony, maybe you just need to explain in more detail why the pony matters.

Our Holy Writing Is Contained in . . .

Once you know what your Word of God(s) say(s), you'll want to put some serious thought into how your wisdom will be contained. How did you answer the quiz in the Introduction?

The Eternal Spirits of the Faithful

This was probably the way our primitive, pre-alphabet ancestors passed the Word on to one another. If it was good enough for them, it should be good enough for you. Let's examine the pros and cons a little.

This oral tradition lends a homey sense of community to your faith, and encourages people to pay attention. It also encourages some creativity. Written works are already open to interpretation. If you add in the unreliability of most peoples' memories, you're going to have to be ready to see your religion "develop" in the retelling. That isn't necessarily a bad thing, unless we repeat it in the next paragraph.

The primary disadvantage to the oral tradition is that it leaves your gospel at the mercy of peoples' unreliable memories, individual creative impulses, and outright willful sabotage. Your faith could very quickly devolve into a giant game of telephone, leaving you recast as the devil, and someone else in charge of the PayPal account, between one spiritual meeting/adoration opportunity/worship service and the next. This solution is best for those of you who don't care if you're in charge of the PayPal account, or for extremely rigid and controlling cults in which you can always hear what everyone else is saying so things can't get too far afield.

An Epic Poem of Enduring Beauty and Grace

This is kickin' it Old School. If you're writer enough to tackle this one, good for you. For most mortal worshipers of anybody or anything, the epic poem is a major undertaking that can sometimes be as hard to read as it is to write. And be ready to spend a lot of time on this one. If it was short, my friends, it wouldn't be called "epic."

The *Mahābhārata*, for instance, which is one of the major Hindu works, is nearly 2 million words long. By comparison, the book you're holding in your hands right now is about 50,000 words. Imagine writing this book forty times over, and with a rhyming scheme, and making it so good people will still be reading it (at least in college-level philosophy classes) in a couple thousand years. Good luck. Most likely you'll end up with . . .

An Epic Poem That's Actually Kind of Over-long and a Little Boring

Believe it or not, there is a significant advantage to doing the epic poem badly: It discourages people from reading it. This is helpful if you—or the gods—change your mind down the road. People won't call you up, saying, "But on line 37, Amon-ra says . . ."

Though it may seem on the surface that you actually *want* your followers to read your holy book, in reality that often doesn't work out. I mean this with all the love and respect I can muster, but when most people get to the salient bits in the Book of Mormon they start rolling their eyes.

If people read your scripture, and love the language of it enough to actually study it, you better be spot on—or at least ready to fend off questions about why it says to stone people who look like your lying, cheating, jackass of an ex-husband in one verse and then admonishes believers not to stone anyone a little later on. Also, it's useful to have some knowledge of science so that you don't accidentally refer to the sun rising in the north or contend that gravity is "just a theory."

If your epic poem sucks, people will just have to take your word for what's in it, like they used to have to do when the overwhelming majority of the population was illiterate. No one reads anymore anyway, frankly, so unless you base your religion on Harry Potter, chances are no one's getting all the way through the book.

If you're a frustrated poet, if your mom is a frustrated poet, if you want to be able to claim that it's all metaphysical/symbolic at a later (court) date, or if you want a good excuse to sit around taking psychedelic drugs for "inspiration," the epic poem might be for you.

This One Book, Which Is the Only Book You'll Ever Need

Because most people fear books, handle them as though they'll be burned if they open them, or just pretend they can't see them, your community of the faithful should be pretty well primed to accept that your book is the only book they'll ever have to read (or more precisely, be read to from) let alone own. Requiring your followers to own said book is a practical means of generating income to help support the lifestyle to which you would like to grow accustomed. Picking a price point can be a bit tricky, though. Check with your local SBA for advice on pricing your products.

In addition to having the Word(s) of (the) God(s) on the pages of the book—which you may wish to refer to as the Book, considering that there will probably be just the one—make sure you have an index so people can quickly and easily find the racy bits (and it absolutely must have some racy bits), and maybe reprint the stuff you really want to drive home somewhere that will stand out even on a casual flip-through. Printing those parts in colored ink, especially red, is always attractive. Or you can also laminate them on cardstock. Cards are preferred by people who would like to have a tangible reminder of their religion but don't know where they would keep a book.

The Ten Commandments, for instance, are the Bible's bullet points, written as though to the corporate vice presidents of Judea. This is definitely something you should think about copying, though calling them commandments may make people think of that other religion. Try to come up with your own name—for example, Laws of [name of your religion here]. Or, try any of these others: "edict," "order," "precept," "rule," "mandate," "stuff you should do." I'm rather partial to "God's Mission Statement." But with contemporary attention spans where they are, you'll want to consider fewer than ten commandments: just the really important stuff—the five or six things that define your religion in its most fundamental form, with an extra one thrown in just for shock value, like the bit about not coveting your neighbor's ass.

The Holy Bookseller

If you can gather enough money from the coven to set up your own publishing house, this can be a lucrative side business for you. If you tell your people they have to have a copy of the Book, someone's got to sell it to them, and it may as well be you.

Publishing can be an expensive proposition, though. Printing costs are killer, and fluctuate with the market-driven cost of paper. Distribution is tough, and expensive, too. With a dwindling number of bookstores out there, and those left making very careful decisions about what they buy, you can have real trouble getting your book on the remaining shelves. And even then, be prepared to soak up returns—the retail book business is essentially 100 percent consignment. You could find that as many as 90 percent of the books you paid to print are eventually destroyed.

But e-books are gaining in popularity at a rapid pace, doubling as an overall segment of the publishing business year over year. E-books are much cheaper to make: no paper, no shipping costs, and the e-retailers are happy for the content for their reader devices. You should consider making the First Caveat, "Thou shalt buy an e-reader, or other device with a free e-reader app." Naturally, the Second Caveat is, "Thou shalt download the Holy Text via Whispernet from Kindle Direct."

Because most people don't know that the little dagger symbol on the *New York Times* bestsellers list means that retailers have reported significant bulk orders, you can buy a bunch for the devoted, then handsell them yourself. If you can swing 100,000 copies, that's usually enough to get you on the list, and from then on you're not just a prophet but a *New York Times* bestselling author, too!

Beatles' Records, Played Backward

This is certainly the second-most effective way of encouraging your flock to interact with your scripture. If you tell followers often enough that if they listen very carefully to "Day Tripper" backward and slowed down to half-speed they'll hear George Harrison clearly reciting the Google Maps directions to your church, *some forty years before that church was even built!* (always make sure that last bit is in italics), well, eventually they're going to think they hear it. Nicer people among the faithful will at least want to humor you, or they may be afraid that the fact that they can't hear it makes them somehow unworthy of your immense grace.

This approach is also relatively cheap and easy. No writing a 2,000,000-word epic poem or having to set up a costly publishing infrastructure. And I doubt the two surviving Beatles will bother to sue you at this point, as though they have nothing better to do.

This is perfect for the cash-strapped start-up religion, and prophets with iffy writing ability.

The Steaming, Bloody Entrails of the Infidels

We'll cover human sacrifice in more detail in Chapter 17, but—oh, I see, you're skipping ahead now. I'll wait.

So now that you've brutally murdered an innocent human victim in the name of your new religion, what do his intestines tell you? Well, that's the beauty of it. If you are the only one who can read them, your cultists are just going to have to trust you that the little swirly bit there is Great Sklootron's way of telling worshipers that the monthly tithe should go up from 15 to 20 percent.

The nice thing about entrails, too, rather than more recognizable oracles such as tarot cards, is that they never seem to spill out the same way twice. It won't matter if the savvy poker players in the cult remember that last time the swirly bit fell that way it meant tithes should go *down*. Just tell them the swirly bit was redder, fattier, and/or more slippery last time. The beauty of this is that it will almost certainly be true.

If you'd rather not risk a felony murder charge, you can study the entrails of animals you've caught in concordance with Holy Law, or you can use roadkill. If that seems really messy, then perhaps reading entrails is not for you and you should stick to reading tea leaves.

Wuss.

CHAPTER 3

Deliver the Most Sacred Rite

give them something to eat, hold,
walk around, step on, etc.

In order for your followers to feel like they're getting something from your new religion, you'll have to develop a whole series of rites and rituals telling them how to do everything from marriage to death. This is very entertaining, so don't stint on the hoop-jumping. We'll get to all of that in Step 3. For now, you need to develop the symbol—the one rite or ritual—that best defines who belongs to your religion. Catholics take communion, your adherents do . . . what?

Your Holiest Rite

To help decide what your holiest rite will be, review your answer to the quiz in the Introduction, the part where you completed this sentence: Our most holy sacred rite consists of . . .

This Really Pretty Flower I Picked This Morning

If you ask people to look for a pretty flower on their way to the temple, won't everyone look nice, walking in holding flowers? That would be sweet. Everyone will feel so pretty holding a flower while reciting the morning prayers to Flori the Flower Goddess that they'll surely come back next week.

But maybe you're not—that is, maybe your God isn't—a flower person. Or maybe you don't want your followers raiding the neighbors' flowerbeds on the way to services. Or maybe you're allergic to all that pollen. Or maybe you find sunflowers creepy. I know I do. That doesn't mean you have to give up on this ritual. Instead, feel free to substitute any found item: stones, loose buttons, or leaves.

Try to find some kind of thematic/story link to your deity. See how that flower thing works for the worshipers of Flori? The Cult of Gvôrg the Merciless might not be quite as flower-friendly. For Gvôrg you might want people to pick up a little stone on the way to the temple that they can throw at the statue of Gvôrg to commemorate the Stoning of the First December, which we all know was that one winter where Gvôrg was captured by the Dexari and stoned for being so merciless. Gvôrg is merciless, and expects no mercy from his followers, so he's happy to be stoned once a week, if only in effigy.

Twinkies

Think of this as a general heading, rather than a specific recommendation. You could use toast, you could use pita triangles, you could use tortilla chips. The key is to have the food item symbolize something. The Catholics use tasteless little wafers to sub in for the metaphorical Body of Christ. Your sacrament can be something similar, but that's such a Catholic thing, really; try to be more original.

What could a Twinkie represent to your adherents? Here are a couple of ideas you might want to copy into your holy writings:

- We eat of the Holy Twinkie to recognize the fallen martyrs of the Looting of the Convenience Stores of Zoobor. Any Zoobor-fearing person knows that story. It was when the evil followers of Dark Alfred raided the sacred convenience stores, leaving behind only the Twinkies. But instead of giving up hope, the Followers of Zoobor made the best of a bad situation and ate the Twinkies. For a million centuries since, the People of Zoobor have eaten Twinkies to celebrate the brilliant ray of hope that lies at the heart of all-loving Zoobor, as symbolized by the golden brilliance of the cake, and the virginal white of the creamy center.

  Could happen.

- It took the seven Gods twelve days to create the universe, and on the fourth day, Greta, Hostess of the Gods, created the Twinkie to pack in the demigods' lunches. Now we end our noon prayers with a Twinkie every weekday because if Greta was kind enough to create it, the least we can do is eat it.

  And we were thankful to have it.

Complex Tea Rituals That Take So Long to Complete the First One Isn't Over Yet

Who doesn't like a nice cup of tea? You can turn teatime into a sacred religious ritual, with acolytes memorizing each step during a long apprenticeship. Your tea will never be served boiled again! If it is, you can make them go back and do it again. If you want to adopt a tea ceremony for your own religion, be careful about simply mimicking the centuries-old Japanese tradition of *Chanoyu,* or one of your followers who has spent an annoying amount of time in the East will immediately point out, "But that's the exact tea ceremony that has been practiced in Japan for six centuries! It can't have been just communicated to you by the Great Hive in the Sky!" Sure, you can excommunicate the heretic but by then the damage will be done. Instead, invent your own tea ceremony based on what you—that is, the Goddess—cares about. If the Goddess likes a lot of honey in her tea, then by all means the Measuring of the Honey should play a large role in your ceremony.

A complex tea ritual will attract wealthy liberals and the wives of wealthy conservatives—people who have nothing better to do. This comes with the built-in advantage that they'll be willing and able to pay exorbitant prices for your tea and ritual serving utensils. The downside is they can be kind of cliquey and pretty soon they're running the religion and telling you your services are no longer required. If you're hoping to appeal to more working-class followers, sub in a quick cup of coffee and let people get back to work.

Pass the Plate

The best ritual tea ceremony will require a special blend of tea that your worshipers can only get from you. Like publishing your own scripture, this is a great side business that can fund temple expansions, retreats, or that hot tub you've always wanted. If you can find a company that will design a special teapot for you, and you can trademark the design, better yet.

A Nice, Lean Piece of Veal

Who doesn't love a nice, lean piece of veal?

Ritual feasts have been a staple of world religions since time immemorial. In 2005, archaeologists in Israel discovered the burial site of a supposed shaman, and five years later uncovered evidence of a burial feast in the shaman's honor—a feast that took place 12,000 years ago. If that's not immemorial, I don't know what is.

If you want to attract adherents to your religion, then having a ritual feast is the way to go. You can make it potluck if you happen to have good cooks among the congregation, or you can have it catered—just remember to include all of the associated setup and cleanup costs when you consider how much to charge.

If you go this route, remember that your followers won't be fully satisfied unless you have some odd dietary laws, such as not eating pickles on Tuesdays or only allowing purple foods on feast days.

Choose this ritual if you hope to someday have either Martha Stewart or Rachael Ray as your celebrity spokesperson.

God(s) Bless Us

Broccoli Dish

Here's a nice recipe for a lovely parve broccoli dish that's Kosher for Passover.
It takes less than an hour to prepare.

IT WILL FEED EVERYONE WHO APPRECIATES EVERYTHING I DO FOR YOU CHILDREN, SITTING THERE NOT EATING LIKE I DON'T KNOW WHAT.

5 cups broccoli

6 eggs

1 cup mayonnaise

1 cup soy milk*

¼ cup matzo meal

2 tablespoons of your favorite Kosher onion soup mix

1. Preheat the oven to 350°F and have your son-in-law, who's so tall, get down the big baking pan. You'll want to spray in a little of that spray stuff so it doesn't stick. Don't say I didn't warn you.

2. In the bowl with the dent in it, because you don't need to have nice things, beat together the eggs, mayo, soy milk, and onion soup mix, then add the matzo meal and beat it some more.

3. Then put the broccoli in the baking pan and pour the mixture over it already.

4. Bake it for 40–50 minutes, until the top is a nice golden brown, like Mrs. Lebovsky when she comes back from Boca.

5. Pray over it.

6. Enjoy. What, you're not eating? You need to eat.

---

*If your religion doesn't have dairy restrictions, use real milk, which tastes better. I mean, let's face it. Soy milk? *Pishachs.*

Blood. And I Don't Mean Figuratively.

As if you need another reason to avoid Lower Manhattan, meet the Court of Lazarus. This vampire cult is open about their blood ritual practice, and even sign agreements to guarantee that the exchange of blood is consensual, and blood is drawn by medical practitioners. The Suri and Masai tribes in Africa drink the blood of cows. TV producers (our generation's high priests) made contestants on *Survivor: Africa* give it a try, too.

Blood rituals are going to be a little off-putting to most people, so if you decide to include blood in your religion, plan on a cult consisting mostly of live-action role-players, as the founders of the Court of Lazarus can surely attest. Most contemporary Americans are deathly afraid of blood, which we know carries horrifying diseases. Even thinking about it can give you a case of Hepatitis I (I for Imaginary, but still, I is one of the incurable ones).

I Can Only Tell You If You Sign This Release First

Native Americans and Pre-Columbian Mexicans have used the hallucinogenic peyote cactus in complex rituals for thousands of years. Some of these trips could go on for two or three days straight. Imagine all the great truths of the infinite universe you can happen upon after about forty-eight hours of wild hallucinations. But the question you'll have to ask is this: Are your religious revelations an effect of the drug's hallucinogenic qualities, and thereby just a figment of your imagination, or does this holy pharmaceutical open your mind up to the Cosmic Truth you're otherwise unable to perceive? Once you have decided on an answer to that, stick to your guns. No one can prove otherwise.

Before you add a potentially dangerous drug to your religion's sacrament, though, be advised that, separation of church and state aside, you will not be able to sell illegal drugs just because God has told you it's okay. Also, when people get really high, especially on powerful hallucinogens like peyote, they have a tendency to see and experience things you weren't prepared for them to see and experience. You may find that your followers trip their way to an entirely new religion of their very own.

CHAPTER 4

What Day Is This?

*who says you can't have
your own calendar?*

Ah, the calendar. It tells you that it's November, and winter is coming on, unless you're Down Under, in which case that's summer you're seeing. It keeps track of how long it takes the Earth to revolve around the sun (or the sun around the Earth, if you're a Republican). It tells you when the feast days are.

We know that God/Goddess/Goat has a sense of humor from the fact that this sun-Earth revolution takes 365.25 days (plus or minus a few minutes), making the math a real bitch.

Calendar Facts

If you are uninterested in facts, you may wish to skip this section. The calendar that the overwhelming majority of the world uses now is ostensibly based on the birth of Jesus, which is said to have occurred on December 25, 1. Basically, this calendar was created by papal decree, originally by Dionysius Exiguus, who, as far as I know, never did fully explain how he knew that Christ was born 525 years before he devised his calendar. Unlike Barack Obama, the Lord has not been pressured to produce a birth certificate, and being born in a manger outside town, and on Christmas, no less, you can imagine the paperwork nightmare.

Suffice it to say that if the pope can create a calendar by fiat, so can you. If you're creating your own religion, don't feel you have to maintain a calendar based on somebody else's religion. Creating your own calendar will be confusing for your followers at first, but there are advantages to having a confusing religion. If people have to keep coming back to you to figure out what day it is, they're more likely to grow dependent on the secret wisdom that only you know.

Several religions still maintain their own calendars, though for practical purposes allow their adherents to use the Gregorian calendar (so-called because Pope Gregory—oh, never mind) to sign their checks. I'm writing this on November 2, 2011, but according to the Jewish calendar, it's Cheshvan 5, 5772. The Islamic Hijri calendar says it's actually 6 Thw al-Hijjah 1432 A.H. And the Old Hindu Lunar calendar says it's Karttika 7, 5112 or just 13 Zac in the Mayan Haab calendar.

If you go by the age of the Earth, it'll be somewhere around the year 4,540,000,000, but if you date back to the Big Bang then it's more like 13,700,000,000. And you thought the Y2K problem was tough, imagine having to rewrite bank software for 11-digit years? No wonder people looked for ways to express time in smaller numbers.

Creating Your Own Calendar

Let's assume you want to start your own calendar. When does your calendar start? What year is it now? (In your religion, I mean. I know what year it is in the usual system, and I hope you do, too.) In the quiz in the Introduction, you were given six choices for what year it is now:

Does Anybody Really Know What Time It Is?
Does Anybody Really Care?

Having no calendar at all can be a little tricky if you're hoping to, say, plan ahead for anything, or look back on anything with any accuracy. But who says you have to do either of those things? Your religion may preach that yesterday is consigned to oblivion as soon as the sun comes up again, so nothing that you remember happening actually happened—that's just the Evil One trying to trick you into the Hell of Consensus Reality.

Doomsday cults sometimes like to plan ahead, but being specific about when the world's going to end can get you in hot water with the cult when that day comes and goes and the Lava Beast at the Heart of the World fails to roast us all alive. If Doomsday might come *at any moment,* what's the point of looking into the future? Is the Lava Beast cooking you right now? No? Okay, then get back to work on those handicrafts we plan to sell on the sidewalk outside the casino.

2012

If you picked the date as 2012, and it is, in fact, 2012, then you are so extremely conventional that you probably don't have the divine spark of creation that will allow you to successfully start your own religion, but don't let me stand in your way. If you chose 2012 and it's actually 2013 or later, you've chosen a strangely nonsensical path, but hey, man, it's your religion.

For Your Consideration

Ooh, wait. What if we went with this? The calendar begins upon first publication of *this book.* I like that one. All human history can then be divided into the time before this book (BB), and the time after it (AB). Sweet. I'm important!

4,256,321,031

The exact, precise figure since the final accretion moment of the infant planet Earth formed from swirling masses of molten rock whirling across the ecliptic plane of the infant solar system, plus or minus a few hundred million years.

If you went with this figure, you've made the decision, whether you were aware of it or not, that your religion is Earth-centric—the creation of the Earth was the most important event in your religion, like the birth of Jesus is to Christians.

That's an important point to keep in mind for all this. Regardless of the moment you begin to count the years, you should have a story about why you started counting *then*. Why is the formation of the Earth important? Or the birth of someone, or the death of someone else, or whatever it is? The day you first decided to start your own religion? The day your 501(c)(3) paperwork came through? Make it a good one, one worthy of the ages.

0

Year Zero has a great, dramatic flair. Though the quiz was asking you if you want it to be Year Zero right now, you'll need to consider the Year Zero question regardless of your numbering system. The Gregorian calendar, for instance, has no zero. It goes from 1 B.C. to A.D. 1, setting aside how people knew that there was only one more year to go before the calendar changed—that matters when you do the math. For instance, Julius Caesar was assassinated in 44 B.C., which, from the perspective of 2012, was 2012+44, or 2,056 years ago. If you throw a Year Zero into the middle of that, it was 2,057 years ago. That might seem like splitting hairs, but hey, you speak for The Infinite. Get it right.

1

Ah, Year One. Why is this the first year? Is it because this is the year you read this book? Flattered! The year you decided to start your religion? Or is it the year you first encountered the Angel Whitney who sang to you of the Revelations of the Overunder beneath a burning sky while stars fell all around you and the lowly creatures of the Earth were given fleeting voice and sang in harmony with the beautiful angel? That sounds more religioney, that last one.

Again, if it isn't specific and rousing in some way, it's probably not worth counting up from. The birth of Jesus was a big deal, as was the creation of the universe, or even the lonely Earth. What immensely huge event happened this year, or is happening now, that makes this the first year of the entire future of the human race?

However Many Years It's Been Since I Was Born

Throughout this book, we'll discuss the pros and cons, in various contexts, of making yourself the focus of your religion. It's been done before, starting, I'm sure, even before the ancient Egyptian pharaohs, who ruled as gods on Earth. Most of the time, when gods manifest on the physical plane, they arrange for some festivities—a little show for the natives. If you want people to start counting the years from your birth, you better be prepared to work a miracle or two.

Though modern technology makes performing miracles a lot easier than it used to be, the fact that everyone knows about technology makes it even harder to get people to believe in miracles. Light shows and burning bushes just make people curious about how you rigged it—ask David Blaine.

Miracles nowadays tend to come in the form of unexpected results and coincidences, like babies surviving earthquakes, or people doing better than a doctor's purposefully conservative, worse-case prognosis (people don't sue their doctors when they do *better* than expected). These sorts of miracles can be a bitch to arrange, but at the same time, people rarely do the sort of background check necessary to debunk stuff they're inclined to believe in.

Want your birthday to be the beginning of the new calendar? Tell your followers you were found in the wreckage of any natural disaster that happened that year. Check out Chapter 11, for the story of my own miraculous rescue!

CHAPTER 5

No One Expects Your Inquisition

for those special moments when you just have to crack some skulls

What happens when one of your people goes off script? What's the use of having a canon/credo/doctrine if the faithful feel empowered to pick and choose their truths? (Repeat after me: "How dare they!") Sometimes, you may find yourself in the position of having to defend the carefully crafted dogma of your new religion against heretics. Simply put, heretics are people who once believed in you but now think your religion is bullshit, possibly because you would not give them a toke on the Pipe of Sweet Dreams. Is there any greater betrayal than to have a formerly faithful believer turn on you? Or question your articles of faith, for example, by demanding that all believers be allowed a toke, rather than just the Elect Few? These are the brothers and sisters who once ate of your Twinkies! Even the most forgiving religious leader has a breaking point.

Dealing with Heretics

Throughout history, religions have tortured and murdered people for heresy. Your religion might not be so militaristic, but then you never know. Religion is a polarizing force, and you *will* lose your temper. It happens to the best of us. Best to be prepared. To that end, consider which tool will be the one you use against heretics:

Surprise

There's nothing like complaining to your cube-mate about your boss only to realize the boss is standing outside the partition, listening to every word you say. As the founder of a new religion, you can sneak up on and surprise potential heretics before they can convert others to their cause. The most efficient way to do this is to enlist a secret police force, charged with eavesdropping on your followers and reporting back to you. Or, you can encourage them to turn each other in for a chance to win a new car, or if you're cash-strapped, a subway token.

Fear

The best way to make sure no one says bad things about you or your religion is to whisper about what happens to people who say bad things about you or your religion. The whispering works best when it doesn't come directly from you, so for best results, you'll want to bribe a few converts into making up wild rumors about that seriously whack thing you did in Vegas.

Ruthless Efficiency

Believe it or not, it is possible to perform an inquisition without actually inflicting torture on someone. In our modern society, assuming your religion doesn't restrict the use of certain technologies, it's possible to investigate a suspect from afar, quietly and methodically gathering intelligence on his or her grievous blasphemies until the threshold of reasonable doubt is passed and the heretic can then be processed through a system regulated by complex rules of due process that eventually lead to a formal trial presided over by an independent judiciary and . . . ah, screw it. Where's that anal pear?

An Almost Fanatical Devotion to the Pope

Here you can simply follow in the Catholic Church's footsteps and deal with heretics the way they once did. No simple excommunication for them! No, no, no! Messy, bloody, painful, and a stain that takes a while to wash off, but who's counting? Another favorite of the Catholic Church is denial, so as you're waterboarding those heretics, you can just smile and wave. It's not torture.

Nice Red Uniforms

The way this works is not everyone gets the nice red uniforms. Only the nonheretics who are assigned to stamp out heresy do. So, in order to get the coveted uniforms, people have to prove their faith by delivering unto you all of the heretics they can find.

All of the Above

This is really the best way to run a religion. Hey, no one said it wasn't going to be mildly upsetting from time to time.

Tools for Rooting Out Heretics

Let's take a look at the actual weapons of the Spanish Inquisition, almost all of which are illegal (except in certain neighborhoods in San

Francisco or downtown Manhattan), so contemporary alternatives are suggested.

Main Weapons of the Spanish Inquisition

The Rack: Currently only used by chiropractors, this was a big flat table on which the heretic was stretched out, wrists and ankles tied to big rollers that the torturer turned way past the comfort point. Though experts disagree as to whether or not anyone ever had his limbs actually torn away, imagine two dislocated shoulders, and two dislocated hips, probably with both elbows and both knees thrown in for the ride. Ouchy.

The Anal Pear: This one had to be messy. An iron device, about the size and shape of a pear, was inserted into the rectum of the offender. Thanks to a clever series of screws, it was made to expand, slowly stretching, tearing, and otherwise causing boo-boos to the unfortunate orifice. Try to explain that one in the security line at the airport.

The Spanish Spider: Reserved for women, this was a nasty set of iron hooks fixed to a woman's breast (it was usually heated first), with the other end chained to the wall. When the inquisitor pulled the woman away, at least some part of her breast stayed with the Spider. That'll learn you to engage in adultery or other horrible sins like, say, being a midwife, or getting fed up with your peasant farmer husband treating you like one of the livestock—or treating one of the livestock like his wife.

Strappado: The inquisitor would tie the accused's hands behind his back, and then tie that to a rope suspended from a pulley attached to the ceiling. When the rope was cranked up by the pulley, the victim's hands slowly rose backward behind his back until his shoulders popped out of their sockets and he was hauled fully off the ground.

Blatant Thievery: Oh, yeah, and while all this was happening, the Inquisition was stealing the victims' personal possessions.

Substitute Weapons

Instead of the Rack ... an advanced Pilates class: This is the perfect method of torture for older or out-of-shape heretics. Considered a form of "exercise," Pilates requires the body to be contorted into an array of unnatural positions, and then held that way under the stern eye of a fierce inquisitor that some fringe cults refer to as a "personal trainer." Five minutes of this, and your enemies will be confessing to the Kennedy assassination.

Instead of the Anal Pear ... the Hardee's Monster Thickburger: This contemporary rectum-wrecker has the added twist of tasting really good going down, but God help us all a few hours later. At approximately 1,420 calories and an absurd 107 grams of fat, it can be served with apple slices instead of fries and still do serious intestinal damage. And this is perfectly legal in all fifty states.

Instead of the Spanish Spider ... the Victoria's Secret Extreme Lift Bra: Anything that touches your skin yet has the word "extreme" in the brand name is probably a bad idea. Though the author is, in general, pro-push-up bra, it's possible that many of these contraptions are simply slower-working versions of the Spanish Spider, mixed with a little of the Heretic's Fork, which was an iron bar that the torturer wedged between the underside of the accused's chin and the upper part of his chest, secured by a neck strap so that it kept the heretic's mouth closed and chin pushed up at an uncomfortable angle. I think you see where we're going with this.

Instead of the Strappado ... Bungee Jumping: Verified by eyewitness accounts and the occasional grainy cell phone video, we now know that there exists in the United States a bizarrely disturbed minority of the batshit insane who delude themselves into believing that tying a giant rubber band to one's ankles and jumping off a really high suspension bridge is a form of recreation. The rest of us understand this to be the single most horrifying thing imaginable, mostly because it's rare that someone dies doing it. If only those seemingly endless seconds of abject terror could be assuaged by the sweet relief of death.

The Least You Need to Know about Inquisitions

Regardless of your chosen method of torture, remember to continuously scream, "Confess! *Confess!*" while inflicting these torments on the unclean, unworthy, or unfunded. And get them to sign over the titles to their cars to you while you're at it.

CHAPTER 6

Sample Religion 1: Scholars of the Particularly Long Book

they who don't get out much

Now that you have some grounding in the basic theory of religion-building, it's time to see how it works in actual practice. In this step, we discuss dogma, so let's take a look at the dogma of the Scholars of the Particularly Long Book.

The SPLB was founded in 1957 when Los Angeles–area medical supply salesman Rick Wemberly, after a year of reading, finally finished L. Ron Hubbard's seminal book *Dianetics*, and said, "Wait. What? *That's it?*"

How Many Gods Are There?

Three.

The Scholars of the Particularly Long Book, as you might have guessed, have at their heart a particularly long book, and like many a work of fiction—oops, I mean, *gospel*—their book is divided into three acts. Each of these acts was created by a different deity, who holds sway over a related, but unique corner of the cosmos. These three deities are:

The Beginning, The Middle, and The End. You can tell they're divine beings, too, because they break the grammar rule about not capitalizing the "t" in "the" in that sort of sentence structure.

The Beginning: She is the goddess of creation, the agent of introduction. It was The Beginning who set the rules for how the universe works, and peopled it with all the stars and planets, flora and fauna, including people. It was She who introduced them to the ongoing story of eternity, establishing where each Character fit into the Eternal Story, and set each and every one of us out on our Sacred Arcs.

The Middle: He is a harsh and unforgiving god, the lord of conflict and plot twists—I mean, *chaos*. The Middle provides each and every one of us with our Burdens and Challenges, forcing us to strive for greatness even as He brings the entire cosmos down upon us in a relentless assault of Dramatic Tension and Rising Action. When you get to The Middle, *anything* can happen!

The End: Neither male nor female, The End is a primal force that reveals to us all, as we approach the final chapters of our lives, the ultimate resolution of our Sacred Arcs. Only The End can choose from one of the two fates that befall all humans, and not until we draw our final breath will we come to know what was chosen for us by The Beginning and relentlessly ground into us by The Middle: Has my life been a Divine Comedy or a Devilish Tragedy?

The Gods Are . . .

. . . Pretty Much Ambivalent about Us, as Long as We're Reading

Expect no love or consolation from either The Beginning, The Middle, or The End. Your Sacred Arc's resolution has been predetermined by The Beginning. The Middle cares not how badly beat up you feel by life—or conversely, how sweet and funny your life might be. And The

End only conjures your Climax, and reveals to you how you have been changed by the story of your life.

Everything that happens in your life was put in place long before you were born. After all, you are a character in the book of everyone else's life, and they are all characters in yours. If all of us had anything like free will, the universe itself would read like a William S. Burroughs novel, and who would want to believe in that?

Our Holy Scripture Is Contained in . . .

. . . This One Book, Which Is the Only Book You'll Ever Need

Behold, the *Particularly Long Book*. As of this writing, the *Particularly Long Book* is up to 4,384,006,410,003 pages, which averages out to about 320 pages for every year the universe has been in existence. The gods alone know how many pages there are left to go—depends on how interesting we are or if it's true about the world ending on the winter solstice 2012. That Mayan Prophecy is part of the ever-evolving story of the universe, so it's just as likely to be true as anything else we've read, heard, or experienced, all of which exists in the *Particularly Long Book*.

Considering the current trade paperback edition of the *Particularly Long Book* has about 280 words per page, and the average person reads about that many words in a minute, it would take almost 92,000 years to read the first 4.4 trillion pages if you literally did nothing but read continuously for twenty-four hours a day, every single day of those 92,000 years. Well, no one is actually expected to finish the thing. After all, it's going to keep going after you die, anyway.

It's the act of *reading* that matters, not *finishing*.

Our Most Important Law Is . . .

. . . Book Open, Eyes Down

Ray Kroc, founder of McDonald's, was famous for the line: "If there's time to lean, there's time to clean." Scholars of the *Particularly Long Book* have their own twist on that: "Unless you're in need, you're expected to read." The SPLB accepts that you have to work for a living, go to the bathroom, help your kids with their homework, and so on, but if it's not something you actually *have to* do, you should be reading. And no, you don't *have to* watch *The Real Housewives of New Jersey*. Turn off the TV and crack that book, Scholar!

Our Most Sacred Rite Consists of . . .

. . . This One Really Long Book and Our Holy Bookmarks

It is absolutely essential that every single Scholar of the Particularly Long Book own a copy of the *Particularly Long Book*. The National Assembly of the Scholars of the Particularly Long Book, Inc., based in Somerville, Massachusetts, holds the exclusive rights to the *Particularly Long Book*. The current version is available by mail-order only for 360 easy monthly payments of only $3,138.00. Unfortunately, the Kindle version is still waiting for a billion-fold increase in overall Internet bandwidth. Once that happens, one person per year will be able to download it, but still the SPLB prefers you order directly from them, for delivery via independent freight company. Waiting a year to download it will just put you a year behind on your reading, after all, and then you'll still have to download a patch for the year you missed. Oh, yeah, and no way will it fit on your iPad.

Scholars of the Particularly Long Book are also expected to have a suitable bookmark. Though there are certain fundamentalists who insist that bookmarks be simple, unadorned slips of acid-free paper, it's becoming more and more popular to show your true devotion with elaborate bookmarks carved from rhinoceros horn, or shaved from the bark of a Nile acacia tree that grows on the site of the Library of Alexandria. A gold-plated bookmark inscribed with your initials is pretty much standard. The SPLB offers a wide variety of bookmarks ranging in price from just $19.99 to the exclusive Swarovski Crystal and James Joyce Pubic Hair Bookmark of Infinite Chapters, which is available at $1,000,000.99 for a limited time only.

Look for coupons in this Sunday's paper, which you're not allowed to read.

What Year Is It? . . .

. . . Does Anybody Really Know What Time It Is? Does Anybody Really Care?

Different people become Scholars of the Particularly Long Book at different times, and have different life demands, so they read at different paces. Though there are on average 320 pages for every year since the universe was first created, some years in there, such as 1983, don't take up that many pages, and other years, such as 57,394,483 B.C., are, like, a thousand pages long. If you live long enough to get to that year, all I can say is . . . *damn*—no way can we all get on the same page.

The SPLB won't start counting the years until the book is finished, and then it'll be expressed in negative numbers. Don't worry, you won't be here to see it.

The Main Weapon of Our Defense Against Infidels Is . . .

. . . This Book

Have you ever been hit in the head with a particularly long, heavy book?

Converts:
So You Don't
Get Lonely

Converts are people who have converted from being converts of one religion to being converts of another religion, hopefully converting from someone else's religion to yours. You can also call them worshipers, members, the devout, the flock, or the faithful.

CHAPTER 7

Save the faithful

*and keep them coming
back for more*

A religion without followers is just a weird guy with strange ideas. Assuming you're the weird guy, you're going to have to get your strange ideas out there to the masses and lure at least a few people into the fold. Competition for the religious life is stiff. It's a crowded field and you'll be competing with some major organizations.

Your Religion as a Start Up

It might help to think of yourself as a struggling little start-up company trying to compete with major corporations for the same customer base. That may not sound any less intimidating, but take heart. Apple and Microsoft were both struggling little start-up companies that eventually beat giants including IBM at their own game. If you start your religion in your garage, like Steve Jobs and Steve Wozniak started Apple, there's every reason to believe that you could eventually face down the Catholic Church.

How?

First, consider the competition and how you can differentiate your religion from the rest. Why would people join you? You need to offer something in return for their faith—a token of your appreciation. You know about grocery stores and their loss leaders? Same concept.

What Does Your Faith Offer?

In the quiz in the Introduction, you were asked this question: What do you have to offer the faithful that no other religion does? How did you answer? If you said "all of the above," then you have covered your bases and will appeal to the vast majority of religion-shoppers. However, sometimes it makes sense to find your niche and exploit that instead. Consider if you want to promise one, some, or all of the following options to potential converts.

Enlightenment

All religions begin with a single organizing principle: I know something you don't. What it is you know that no one else does is entirely up to you, but unless you have some impenetrable secret, your religion is a nonstarter. When you have a secret only you and God/Goddess/ Goat know, people will come to you for that information, so you better make sure your secret is really enlightening or they won't come back. Examples of enlightening secrets include:

- The entire universe is contained in a single atom on the tip of the toenail of Brovex the Ginormous.
- God has been waiting for an eternity to finally perfect the human race, and I am the first of the new generation of perfect humans (can't you tell?).

- If you look into a mirror with the lights off and say "Bloody Mary Hawkins" three times she'll appear in the mirror and show you her boobs.
- Keanu Reeves is gay.
- The solar system will come to an explosive end on May 23, 2133 when José Jimenez of Juarez, Mexico, finally satisfactorily answers the question, "What is the meaning of life?"

Eternal Life

People don't like death. The problem is, it's out there waiting for us all, even those of us who eat fat-free salad dressing. Most religions have addressed this by finding some way to make people feel better about dying, mostly by convincing them that they're not really dying, they're just going to another life in a better place. Because people are predisposed to want to believe this, as the alternative is nonbeing in a great howling void, by offering eternal life as a feature of your religion you can easily attract many converts. Think carefully about what your religion has to say about death and the Great Beyond. It may be hard to believe, but there are some ridiculous ideas out there already. We'll get into that more in Step 5.

Contentment

People who are sane prefer pleasure to pain, but unless you plan to have sexual orgies feature largely in your ceremonial rites (see "Sex" to follow), you will need to find another way to offer pleasure to potential converts. "Contentment" is one excellent option. It has no salacious undertones that could lead to disappointment ("Hey, I thought there would be nudity").

Note: If you feel that your niche is to cater to the *in*sane, then you'll want to avoid any appearance of your religion offering "peace," "contentment," "tranquility," or any synonym thereof. Skip to the next section.

Many people find life confusing, overwhelming, and, well, hard. If you offer them the promise of contentment, they will be inclined to give your religion a go. A very nice spin on this premise is offering them the promise of contentment if they work really hard, thus allowing the highly suspicious ("you don't get something for nothing, sonny!") to be reassured that it must be true, as it doesn't sound too good to be true.

Revenge

The motorist who cut you off in traffic, the little red-haired girl who married someone else, the boss who stole all the credit—wouldn't it be nice to get a little revenge? And not get thrown in jail for it? If you promise people that the gods will take revenge for them, you'll have converts lining up at your door in no time.

However, if your god is a vengeful god, you'll have to be careful to make sure that god isn't looking for revenge on the people you're trying to attract to your services. If God is looking for revenge on *other* people, that's usually fine. If you can figure out how to arrange it so God is out for revenge against people who have wronged the people you're trying to attract, that's best.

Sex

Sex is the one thing everybody wants to have and you can attract followers, especially teenagers, by promising them they can have it. Humans, being mammals, are hard-wired for sex and will go to great lengths to get it. You can capitalize on that biological imperative by either trying to get people to control their predilection for sex, in the interests of protecting them from the consequences (babies, enraged spouses, sexually transmitted diseases, political disgrace) or you can be a proponent of free love, e.g., you can offer sexual orgies on fixed occasions, in exchange for their faith. How often these sexual orgies take place will depend, in part, on your sex drive because you will have to supervise. (No one said starting a religion didn't require long hours at the office and a certain amount of personal sacrifice.)

Some people cannot enjoy sex unless it's forbidden, so you may wish to consider placing restrictions on sex in order to enhance the experience for your followers. See Chapter 19 for ways to do this.

Getting Followers

People don't always "shop" for religions in the same way they shop for computers, cars, or other consumer goods. Most people are brought up in a particular faith and stay there for the rest of their lives. But there are people who do shop for religions, who bounce from faith to faith for all sorts of reasons, including fashion. These people are your first layer of potential converts. The rest will follow.

To convince that first group of converts to join you, you have to make your religion fashionable. Finding a celebrity spokesperson (see Chapter 8) can be an excellent start. Or, you can focus on a core group of hipsters in your local area before branching out. Try coffee shops, or hang around the beer aisle at the grocery store and strike up a conversation with anyone who picks out a six-pack of Pabst.

Remember: Someone, somewhere right now is dissatisfied with his/her/its faith. These people are potential converts. You just have to find them.

Promotional Strategies

Here are some useful ideas for ways you can spread the word. Keep this list close at hand and check these off as your resources allow.

Flyers

Still the cheapest, easiest form of advertising, flyers can be handwritten if you still don't have enough in the collection plate for a computer. You can make flyers that just spread the truth as you see it, but it's best if they include what advertising executives refer to as a "call to action." Are you having some kind of event—a potluck, a rummage sale, or a virgin sacrifice? Make sure your flyers tell people when and where that's taking place. Have regular services? Great—when and where?

Make as many copies as you can afford, but check your local ordinances before distributing them. Sticking them under car windshield wipers may be legal in one spot but considered misdemeanor littering across the street. Hand them out on the street, and post them on community bulletin boards at supermarkets and coffee houses. Ask local retailers and restaurants if they'll put your flyer in the window, and be courteous when they say no. Creating the flyer can be fun, but distributing it is going to take some work. If you already have a few converts, tell them that converting others is an act of faith and earns them brownie points with the Big Guy/Gal/Goat.

Pamphlets or Brochures

Many online services can help you create professional-looking three-panel pamphlets or brochures, and if you have reasonable computer skills you can make them yourself and have them printed at the local Kinko's. Pamphlets should be more general than flyers—not tied to a particular event, but something you can use for a long time, even years. A pamphlet allows more space for text—a chance for you to really get the word out there. If you can find a mailing list, and can gather the money for postage, you can mail these out to potential followers, too.

The Sign at the Edge of Town

Drive out of town, then turn around and drive back in. Does your town have one of those "Welcome to . . ." signs with smaller signs hanging under it? If so, you might see churches mixed in there among the fraternal organizations. Contact your town's chamber of commerce, or just go to your city hall, and find out how to get your church added to that sign. It will lend you instant credibility.

A Van

Find a reliable used van with a few rows of bench seats, paint the name of your church on the side, and drive around picking people up for services. A lot of people out there, especially old people, would be delighted to come to your services, but can't get there on their own. God forbid their sons, who live just down the street, bother to come over and drive them to church, but don't worry about them, they'll be fine. Used utility vans can be had for a song, and if you don't have enough left in the collection plate for a professional paint job, just do it yourself. Even if you're not a talented artist, people are suckers for the whole "grass-roots" thing. If it's obvious you did it yourself, out of love and devotion to the cause, that's actually better than anything too slick and overly commercialized. And don't be shy about using the van—drive it every-where. It's a rolling billboard.

Billboards (Nonrolling)

If you can distill the Truth down to a few words, get those few words up over the highway. You'll need money for this, and you'll have to choose your location carefully, but a giant roadside sign that says GOD HATES YOUR ENEMIES! or LIVE FOREVER IN PARADISE— ASK ME HOW! (with your 800 number, of course), can really drag 'em in on a Sunday.

Radio

It used to be that radio was the principal form of mass media, but the generation that remembers those days is mostly gone. Now, radio is split into three competing camps: background music for dentists' offices, sports, and crackpots. No offense or anything, but unless your religion is sports-based you're going to be in the last category. Try not to be put off by that—some of these raving maniacs have huge followings, and those huge followings attract substantial advertising revenues.

Television

Even in the Internet age, TV remains the most powerful force in the world, and televangelists are the wealthiest religious leaders outside the Vatican. If you can get on TV... *damn*. But competition is fierce, so unless you're already working from a deep wellspring of capital and can just buy time—a lot of religious programs on TV are essentially infomercials—you'll need a way in, and that way in is the cable-access show. Contact your local cable company and see if this is something they still do. If not, consider protesting some issue or another, even one that has nothing to do with religion, such as the city's move to place recycling bins outside city hall, so that you can get picked up on the local news.

The Internet

In the twenty-first century, if you don't have a website, you don't exist. At the very least, make sure your church has a Facebook page and a Twitter account. Both of those are free and can help you build a network of followers. Of course, because they're free, everyone else has one, too, so floating to the top of that immensely crowded field can take considerable effort and lots of time. But you have to stick with it. Make sure you update your Facebook page daily and Tweet as often as you can. Pack as much Truth as possible into your 140 characters and always end with a hash tag such as #theendisnear or #ispeakforgod.

CHAPTER 8

God Helps Those Who Have Celebrity Spokespeople

*who wouldn't believe
a movie star?*

Imagine the flood of converts who will crowd the temple steps after Tom Cruise jumps up and down on Oprah's couch proclaiming his love of your enduring wisdom. Tom Cruise will be contractually tied up with Scientology for a while, and Oprah has retired the couch, but still, celebrity endorsement opportunities abound.

Celebrities speak at religious gatherings, tout books and personal appearances by religious leaders, and write books of their own about how their religion saved their lives, whitened their teeth, and inspired their latest CD, which drops Tuesday.

Using Celebrity Spokespeople

There have been a number of inspiring stories of celebrities from various media who have taken either the religion of their upbringing or their conversion to a new faith out into the limelight in positive ways, even if mean, cynical people sometimes make fun of them. If you can get a celebrity to support your new religion, you'll be in great shape.

Here are a few examples of celebrities who have done the religious spokesperson thing right:

Muhammad Ali
(The Greatest Boxer of All Time)
Muslim

Cassius Clay was already a boxing sensation when he announced his conversion to the Nation of Islam, a Muslim group that recruited disenfranchised African Americans throughout the 1960s and '70s. Despite the Nation of Islam's often troubled relationship with the law, Ali, his violent occupation aside, seems to have led a life of spirituality and peace since his conversion, even sticking to his convictions enough to refuse induction into the army during the Vietnam War, which the Nation of Islam (and lots of other people) opposed. That was a costly decision for him, but is a significant reason why Muhammad Ali serves as a positive role model for people all over the world to this day.

Richard Gere
(*People* Magazine's Sexiest Man Alive, 1993 *and* 1999)
Buddhist

Though his call for peace and reconciliation got him booed at a post-9/11 charity event, Richard Gere does the whole Buddhist thing with a great deal of class. Buddhism is a particularly peaceful and contemplative religion that's certainly at odds with the default lifestyle of the Hollywood movie star. This is a guy women adore. He can have sex with any woman he wants to, whenever he wants to.

Come to think of it, that's probably why he's so chill.

Bill Maher
(Late Night Talk Show Host)
None of the Above
Though it has become acceptable to be stridently anti-Muslim in the United States since 9/11, no other religious minority is more openly reviled than the people who reject religion entirely. Bill Maher has not only come out of a closet that most American atheists inhabit by necessity, he never shies away from an opportunity to get his message out on his own show, and any other show that will have him. That takes balls.

Finding a Celebrity Spokesperson

Finding a celebrity can be tough, especially so-called "A-list" celebrities. A-List celebrities are actors whose names appear onscreen before the title of the movie, rock stars who play stadiums instead of clubs, and athletes you recognize on sight even though you don't live in the city they play for. Celebrities dip in and out of the A-list depending on the success of their last few ventures. You might have a better chance of attracting celebrities in their moments of weakness. Your window for getting Ben Affleck, for instance, may be closing, but Harrison Ford is still pretty well up for grabs.

Some celebrities look to religion as a way to repair damaged reputations and get back in the public's good graces. If you can find that clinic where they shoot the VH1 show *Celebrity Rehab* and hang around in front—use the time to hand out flyers or sermonize via megaphone—you might snare a post-hottie like Brigitte Nielsen or maybe the drummer from Guns N' Roses. There's little chance any of them will be on the A-list again anytime soon, but if you preside over their inevitable funeral you'll get a few minutes' national cable news exposure. And you can get them cheap.

Sometimes your celebrity spokesperson can go off the reservation and do you more harm than good. Managing their egos and addictions can be difficult, time-consuming, and expensive, and they can be harder to cut loose from the flock than a sixty-five-year-old spinster. Here are a few examples of celebrity spokespeople you might want to avoid:

Mel Gibson

(*People* Magazine's Sexiest Man Alive, 1985)

Catholic

The only difference between Mel Gibson now and Mel Gibson in 1979 is that in 1979 he was only pretending to be the sole survivor of a worldwide apocalypse (most likely the fault of the Jews) who lives a life of violence, revenge, and reckless driving. When he was rich, famous, faithful to his wife, and a stern disciplinarian to his 843 children, Mel Gibson was the Catholic Church's dream spokesman. Then he was pulled over in L.A. and went on a wild, raving, drunken, anti-Semitic rant and his career was towed to the impound yard, where it still languishes.

Hmm. Maybe Jews really are in control of Hollywood. If he'd blamed all wars on atheists he'd be a senator now.

Tom Cruise

(*People* Magazine's Sexiest Man Alive, 1990)

Scientology

For a while there, Tom Cruise was so A-list he'd passed up even the A-list to inhabit some level of mega-ultra-superstardom reserved only for him. Then he jumped all over Brooke Shields for taking anti-depressants, yelled at Matt Lauer on the *Today Show*, and walked on Oprah Winfrey's furniture with his shoes on. *South Park* made a joke of

Scientology's creation myth, dragged a cartoon version of Tom Cruise through some of the goofier stuff, and all of a sudden, *poof!* no more Tom Cruise. Well, that wasn't all *South Park's* doing. The title *Mission: Impossible* was supposed to describe the mission the fictional spies were on, not the audience's efforts to understand what the heck was going on.

Madonna
("Singer")
Kabbalah
Really?
I know, right?

Stephen Baldwin
(Guy Who Calls in to Fox News Shows)
Evangelical Christian
Always a lesser Baldwin, Stephen is the internationally famous star of such films as *Shark in Venice* and *Shoot the Duke*. Probably just to piss off his openly liberal big brother Alec, Stephen drank the Born Again Kool-Aid and then some, to become more famous (if that's the right word) for taking the neoconservative/theocratic side on third-rate conservative rant shows. Something tells me the overwhelming majority of Christians would rather he just shut the fuck up.

Charlie Sheen
(Former TV Star)
Winning
There is literally not a single human being on Planet Earth that I would rather bought this book than Charlie Sheen. If he could take what's written here and tell us how to come to his church to gain the

power of Adonis DNA and Tiger Blood I will be first in line. He's already had a couple of goddesses, so he's past Chapter 1 at least.

You as Celebrity

Some of you may be thinking that *you'll* be the celebrity spokesperson for your new religion. After all, some founders of new religions, such as L. Ron Hubbard (Scientology) or Joseph Smith (Mormonism), were very well known in their time, and are still admired by their followers today. However, bear in mind that some founders of new religions include Jim Jones, David Koresh, and Charles Manson.

Stop and think, very carefully, if you want to be anywhere near that company. You may be better off behind the scenes, where your followers can quietly shepherd you off to treatment should incipient megalomania take hold.

CHAPTER 9

Unleash the fanatics

or rein them back in

Fanatics can be your religion's best friends—or worst enemies. Imagine people who will do your bidding without question! Think of the good they could do! Or, you know, the death and destruction they could wreak.

Fanatics can be good for business. They'll tirelessly promote your religion, fill your coffers, and wash your windows. You could even marry one and get your mom off your back. Those are good fanatics, the kind you want. What you don't want is the kind that makes the local sheriff call you up after services every Tuesday, saying, "We've got more of your fanatics here in lockup. You planning to come bail 'em out?"

Good fanatics start with your dogma and scripture, but then take it to the next level, a place reserved only for the super-faithful. When you notice someone's achieved this level of devotion, be sure to reward him/her/it.

Inducements for Fanatics

To help converts become fanatics, you'll want to offer special deals to them. The seventy-two virgins thing already has a been-there, done-that quality to it, so if you're looking to motivate fanatics you'll need to come up with enticements of your own. Consider some of these handy carrots:

Fanatic Inducement Checklist

○ A Coupon for a Free House
Present this coupon between April 1, 2013 and May 1, 2013 and you'll get the keys to this beautiful single-family home on a secluded two-acre lot close to shopping. Schaumburg schools! Oak cabinets. Nontransferable.

That last bit, "nontransferable," is important, because you're going to send them out on their suicide missions before April 1, 2013 and you don't want their heirs trying to cash in on that house, which you don't actually have, of course.

○ Seventy-two Porn Stars
This takes all the vagaries and interpretation out of that virgin thing. After all, wouldn't you rather spend eternity with people who know what they're doing?

○ An X-box 360 with All the Games
This is kind of a cruel joke, too, because you know the 360 is going to be obsolete long before eternity is over. Your fanatics will be sitting there like assholes playing *Assassin's Creed* while the Virtual Real-

ity Direct-Neural Interface X-box 360,000,000 players are really assassinating people.

○ 20,000 Bonus Miles
You'd be surprised what people are willing to do for 20,000 bonus miles—and I mean absurd things like use their credit cards to buy gas, or subscribe to *Travel & Leisure* magazine.

Identifying the Fanatics in Order to Use Them

Fanatics can sometimes be difficult to spot. The line between the faithful and the dangerously faithful can sometimes be a fine one. Here's a short list of handy tips that I like to call, "You might be a fanatic if . . ."

- you line up a month early for Sunday Service
- your copy of the holy book has several pages "mysteriously" stuck together
- you're already sending out invitations to *next year's* Holiest Holiday party
- someone can snap his fingers an inch in front of your face and you don't blink
- you don't get embarrassed when someone catches you talking to yourself
- you show up to worship with a sleeping bag
- you possess bombs of any size or description

Discouraging Fanaticism

If you'd rather not have the fuss and bother of dealing with fanatics, then you'll want to start a religion that doesn't encourage fanaticism. For example, you could become a branch of the Methodists. Fanatics are drawn to absolutes. They cause trouble when they're told that a certain group of people or set of behaviors is so inimical to their religion that it's not only okay but essential that they act out violently, or do other weird stuff that makes people uncomfortable or could have a negative impact on society, such as following Sarah Palin's tour bus or calling in to vote on *American Idol* more than once a week.

Reining in Your Fanatics

If the sheriff does, from time to time, call you of a Tuesday evening, then you may need to rein in your fanatics. You may need to set constructive goals for them. For example, if you do not want them burning other people's temples, then task your fanatics with handing out pamphlets at the subway station.

Remember, a bored fanatic is a fanatic who starts Googling "how to build bombs." Instead, instruct your fanatics in origami, or teach them to memorize all the verse in Browning's *The Ring and the Book*.

Another option is to loan them out to the local crime boss for a generous "consideration."

CHAPTER 10

March Off to the Holy Wars

*at least threaten to, anyway,
from time to time*

Holy wars are about trying to get infidels (defined as anyone who doesn't belong to your religion) to do what you want because you can't get them to do it in a peaceful way—or maybe you just want them dead. Of course you would never do such a thing if God/Goddess/Goat didn't want you to, so your holy writings will have to be clear on the subject, while still giving you at least limited war powers.

You never know . . .

Great Moments in Holy Warfare
November 27, 1095

Pope Urban II gives a rousing address in the French city of Clermont, calling on Christendom to reclaim the Holy Land from the Muslim Arabs. The speech is interrupted by shouts of *Deus lo volt!* (God wills it!), and the Crusades are on like Donkey Kong.

Taking a Position on Holy Wars

In the quiz in the Introduction, you were asked this question: "When is the best time to fight a holy war?" This will help you decide the best strategy for dealing with provocations that occur. If, for example, you chose "Never," then even if the school secretary makes a scheduling mistake and you have to have your Holiest of Holy Services in the boy's locker room rather than the cafeteria, you will accept that indignity with, er, dignity. If, on the other hand, you believe that no one actually stops fighting a holy war, then you know what to do.

Never

If you chose "Never," you'd better make sure your holy writings, chants, hymns, and whatnot are crystal clear on the subject. Maybe start every temple invocation with, "War is bad for flowers and other living things." Or have your fanatics light themselves on fire outside of army recruiting offices.

Lighting *oneself* on fire isn't, by definition, an act of war.

If You're Absolutely Sure You Can Win

Also known as the Bush Doctrine, this is good advice for people who are too busy to form a set of ethical and moral values to guide their lives and moderate their transitory outbursts of temper. If you answered this way, you're okay with hurting people to get ahead, but not okay with risking being hurt back. This sort of thing usually starts with the collection of lunch money.

Before All That Sarin Gas You Bought from That North Korean Guy Expires

Take the "sell by" date on this stuff seriously. It's expensive and hard to handle so you want to make sure you get the most number of kills per cylinder.

Chemical and biological weapons can be difficult to manage, in general, and hard to get your hands on, but there are home-grown versions you might want to consider. If some of the kids in your congregation come down with chickenpox, have them sneak into the competing temple and lick stuff. Or stock up on semi-legal fireworks over the Fourth of July holiday, tie all the fuses together, then leave a lit cigarette so that it'll act as a timer. If you set this up in your enemies' bathroom, they'll get a real surprise at the next ice cream social when the initial bang is followed by a plumbing-assisted biological assault.

After the Thirteenth Solstice Before the End of the Great Migration of Givornius

I mean, what? Are you supposed to start the holy war after the *twelfth* solstice before the end of the Great Migration of Givornius? Dude. That's just crazy talk.

When Someone Steps to You

Some religions have tried to build in safeguards against violent retribution, preaching patience and forgiveness. It doesn't usually work, though, and sometimes, well, you end up with the Israeli army, and you need to think twice before you step to them, dog.

A good offense starts with a good defense. At least, that's what you want to say when someone (like a new convert, or an ATF agent) asks you about the weapons stockpile in the basement. Just because you won't shoot first and ask questions later doesn't mean you can never shoot at all. Allow one of your followers to become a martyr, then open fire!

Wait, Who Says You Can *Stop* Fighting a Holy War?

There is historical precedence for this sort of thing. The Crusades went on for centuries, on and off, and some people think they're still going on right now, even if under slightly different banners, and over slightly different resources. If you're one of those "shoot constantly, ask questions never" types, you're probably going to attract a following of deeply disturbed individuals, or people who thought you were talking about a video game. If you end up with more of the latter, your holy war is going to fizzle. People play violent video games because they're afraid of violence in real life, whereas truly violent people are too busy beating each other up in bars to find the Eclipse Easter Egg in *Call of Duty*.

The idea of a never-ending war, as popularized by political masterminds such as George Orwell and Dick Cheney, can be a powerful recruiting tool, and keep the faithful in a state of constant readiness. What better reason to increase the monthly tithe by 5 percent, or demand more high-end electronics for the temple rummage sale, than a sudden setback on the eastern front? Anyone who hesitates is obviously a heretic insurgent.

Great Moments in Holy Warfare

April 6, 1896

There's some controversy on the exact date, but this is the widely accepted first meeting of the Cougars of Brigham Young University and the Utes of the University of Utah—a conflict that has come to be known as *The* Holy War. So far, no reports of bombings or massacres have come in from Utah, but we will continue to keep an eye on this hyper-ritualized ground acquisition contest fought hand-to-hand by armored warriors.

Sample Religion 2: The Church of Phil

the gospel according to Me

People keep telling me, "Phil, you are like unto God," and when I say, "Yeah, I know, thanks, man," they usually counter with, "What? I didn't say anything," but I heard it. They can't fool me.

That being the case, I hereby proclaim the birth of the new One True Faith, the Church of Phil.

I have a leg up on finding converts: this book. See, you're getting my Message right now, subconsciously getting used to my Sacred Capitalizations, which will begin to create new associations in your mind. Can you feel Me in there yet? I know you can.

But this book alone won't do it, so I made up a flyer:

Converts to the Church of Phil, known as Philites, receive many Gifts from the Great Phil, but chief among these is a mixture of Enlightenment and Contentment, because Phil doesn't think you can have one without the other. See how Phil is already starting to refer to Himself in the third person? That gives the impression that Phil is Greater even than Phil Himself.

A Note on "Philites"

What are your followers called? People like to identify themselves with words such as Buddhist, Taoist, or Mormon. It's always less confusing if you figure out some variation on the name of your religion, like I did with the Church of Phil. If you worship the Twelve Gods of the Convergence of Hazblidan, for instance, your worshipers could be called Hazblidites, Hazblidans, Hazblidolians, Hazblidists, etc.

The holy scripture of Phil is contained in all the books written by Phil, including *The Guide to Writing Fantasy and Science Fiction,* available now from Adams Media, wherever fine books are sold. To truly serve Phil, thou shalt buy His books, read them, and render unto Amazon a Positive Review. Go forth, children, and evangelize!

It is only through the purchase of the Books of Phil that you will achieve enlightenment. The Truth is contained in those pages, along with some awesome fight scenes. Ponder well and deeply the Words of Phil, and when you have posted five-star reviews of all His Great Works, you will feel the Waves of Contentment wash over you. I promise. I mean, *Phil* Promises.

Phil is still looking for the right celebrity spokesperson but has already identified Charlie Sheen as an ideal candidate. He combines the right degree of handsomeness and insanity that can really get you noticed. Phil would also very much like to sit down and talk religion with Sofia Vergara, who plays Gloria on ABC TV's *Modern Family*, because Phil, let's say, "respects her as an artist," and believes she would make a good Sister Wife. That last bit will still have to be approved by the Holy Wife of Phil, who is the True Power behind the throne. Phil doesn't think it looks good, but it's worth a try.

It is assumed that all of the Philites are fanatics, and Great Phil sees them as His "core audience." If you're not fully committed to the Church of Phil, there's a nice Methodist church down the street. Phil needs people who are willing to read His books, and that requires serious devotion.

Phil would prefer not to fight a holy war of any kind, but Phil will admit that He's not 100 percent ready to dismiss answer D, "After the thirteenth solstice before the end of the Great Migration of Givornius," because Phil still has some hard feelings about something that happened in junior high, which Philites know as "The Dark Times." And the thirteenth solstice is coming up next year, so, now or never.

In Chapter 4, Phil promised to tell you what year it is, among the Philites, and here goes:

It is the year 48 P.P. (post-Phil) or will be until next year. Phil was born in Rochester, New York, in September 1964 but found alive and well in the rubble of the Olympia Earthquake, some 3,000 miles away in the Seattle area, on May 6, 1965, a full seven days after the April 29, 1965 quake. Phil was only eight months old. How did Phil even get from Upstate New York to Washington State? How did Phil survive for seven days without food or water? It was a miracle! And that's why Phil now lives near the site of that defining moment of supernatural supernaturalness, and from Here Phil doth Spread the Word!

Ritual: So You Have Something to Do

A ritual is pretty much anything you do over and over in more or less precisely the same way. For instance, people have a "morning ritual," which describes the order in which they brush their teeth, eat breakfast, and get dressed. Your religion also needs rituals. People expect them and like having something to do, especially if it's something that could curry favor with the Big Guy/Gal/Goat. In this step, you'll learn the myriad ways to use ritual in your religion.

CHAPTER 12

Establish Your Shrine, Mega-Church, Fane, or Other Temple

*because you have to
meet somewhere*

First things first. You have to have a place to perform your rituals before you get out the knife/prayer beads/peyote. If you've ever watched or participated in someone else's religion, you know that houses of worship can range from the humble (Billy Bob's Church of Christ and Bait Shop) to the magnificent (the Parthenon). Though you may not have the financial resources of the Egyptian pharaohs, take heart. Some of the best religions have started out small, only to achieve world domination in a matter of time. Plus, later in this chapter we'll look at ways you can get your followers to foot the bill for you. Sweet, right?

Your House of Worship

The quiz in the Introduction asked, "Where do you plan to hold your sacred rites and ceremonies?" The answer = your house of worship. If you're undecided on the best choice for your religion, please consider the following pros and cons of each approach.

The Whole World Is Our Shrine

This is a good one, as it takes all the expense and complexity of real estate out of the equation right up front. If the whole world is your church you can hold services, perform weddings or sacrifices, and otherwise do what you do pretty much anywhere: in a meadow, near the levee, in the parking lot of EZ Finance Used Cars. Here's an idea: Only hold your services outside when it's sunny. If the Seven Gods of the Rainbow Pantheon want you to pray to them today, they'll make sure the sun's out. Otherwise, you're off the hook. If yours is a religion of suffering, you'll want to go the other way: Only hold services during inclement weather.

The problem with the whole world being your church is that it takes a measure of control out of your hands. If you only pray when it's sunny, what happens if there's a long cloudy spell? You don't want your followers going too long without at least touching base with them. And people tend to be homebodies. We build buildings and live in houses because we like them, not only because we need shelter. If religion is at least a little bit about control, you'll find you have more control over the inside of some kind of building—any kind of building—than you ever will over the natural world.

Usually in the Living Room, but Lately It's Been Kinda Spilling over Into the Kitchen

Why not make your religion a home-based one? You're already paying the overhead, plus you don't have to fight traffic to get there. If you're thinking of going the cult route, this is a particularly useful choice because you want your cultists living with you, the better to ensure their complete acceptance of your teachings. Also, you can convince them that keeping your place clean and your kitchen stocked is an act of faith.

You may never have to go grocery shopping again. If you end up with a lot of acolytes living with you, then you may have to move to larger quarters, but the key here is to have your followers sign over their life savings to you before they move in. If they do, you should be able to swing the rent at least until it's time to meet the UFOs.

Of course, having your cultists living with you 24/7/365 has its downsides. People who live together end up breaking down a lot of personal barriers. Your cultists will see you coming in and out of the bathroom. They might see you naked. They might find the hidden stash of books, magazines, or DVDs that you've told them they can't see but that you still every once in a while take a peek at. They'll wake you up in the middle of the night with philosophical questions, and without fail, one of them will insist on bathing herself in patchouli. There's something to be said for everyone going to his or her separate corners from time to time.

We Rent the Middle School Gym, Except During Basketball Season

All sorts of public spaces are available to rent in communities across the country, including the middle school gym. With just a little research and a few phone calls you should be able to find exactly the right-size room for the number of converts you have. Some places, including hotels and convention centers, can even provide catering, lighting and sound equipment, and photocopying services. They may not take too kindly to human sacrifice, but then, especially in these troubled economic times, you might be surprised what you can get someone to pretend not to see for a couple of extra shekels.

On the other hand, the Arizona Room at the local Marriott lacks a certain ceremonial majesty. Let's be honest, the Sistine Chapel it ain't.

You might also find that you're in a ballroom next door to another religious gathering, and if they seem to be having more fun, you might lose converts as they trickle off to the Naked Dancing Coven next door in the Oklahoma Room. And if you're the leader of the Naked Dancing Coven, no way are you going to be able to hold your sacred rites in the school gym, at least not more than once.

A Sweet Little Temple on a Hill

Unless you're coming into this with some capital reserves, your own little temple on a hill is something you're going to have to save up for. I'd advise using your first round of tithes to have an architect draw up a sketch of your building, and maybe make a little model. You can bring this to your living room, or to the middle school gym, and rally the faithful around raising funds for its construction. Make sure you poll the congregation for people who might be able to provide carpentry services on a volunteer basis.

Even a modest building can be expensive, and then there are location issues, permits, and all sorts of other stuff you have to worry about. You might want to consider renting or buying an existing building and converting it to your faith. Still, that can be expensive in its own right. Don't just look for a contractor among the faithful, but also a good real estate agent and maybe someone from the local building department.

A Massive Cathedral with Flying Buttresses and Other Architectural Elements That Sound Vaguely Dirty

The concept of the ridiculously huge and overly impressive, insanely expensive mega-church, which first began with the building of the great Gothic cathedrals in twelfth-century Europe, is alive and well in contemporary America. The biggest church in the United States is Joel

Osteen's Lakewood Church in Houston, Texas, which seats 16,800 people. It cost more than $75 million so this is not a "starter church." Take heart, though; the Lakewood Church began in an abandoned feed store.

Before you build a temple for 16,800 people, you should have at least, say, 10,000 really committed followers who you know will show up on the first day. Sinking nine figures into a cathedral only to have a few dozen cultists filter in and out every week is just going to make you look bad, whereas that same number of people will fill the abandoned feed store to capacity.

The mega-church also puts you on the hook for a massive monthly overhead. Imagine the electric bill on a 16,800-seat arena. But then if you can reliably fill all those seats, and everybody only tithes, say, $100 a month, you're looking at a cool $20 million a year in (partly tax-free) income.

Where do I sign up?

A Stepped Pyramid Decorated with the Blood of Sacrificial Virgins, and Kick-ass Metallica Posters

The neighbors may not like it, but if they bitch, sacrifice them. In the meantime, make sure you memorize this:

"Congress shall make no law respecting an establishment of religion, or prohibiting the free exercise thereof; or abridging the freedom of speech, or of the press; or the right of the people peaceably to assemble, and to petition the Government for a redress of grievances."

That 200-watt stereo is part of your sacrament, dude. Crank it.

Still, you're going to have to expect that you'll be in court for a certain portion of each year, and legal fees can be a real killer. Also, because it is actually against the law to sacrifice anyone, including virgins, the Constitutional argument will only take you so far.

If you build your pyramid out of strong enough material, and fill it with supplies, you could conceivably hold out in there, eating the flesh of the unworthy (e.g., people who want to give themselves up), for weeks or even months on end.

Oh, and your pyramid can have smooth sides if you prefer.

What to Call Your Temple

Churches, temples, synagogues, and other houses of worship have all sorts of creative names. You can name your temple after important followers, saints, or contributors. If someone in the congregation ponies up a $100,000 contribution surely you can name at least a part of the building after him, like the Bill Johnson Narthex, or the Juanita Gonzalez Vestibule.

If you've got the connections, you can try for a corporate sponsorship. Sports teams do it, why not you? If there can be a Century Link Field in Seattle or a Lucas Oil Stadium in Indianapolis, why not the F+W Publications Holy Library of the Particularly Long Book, or the Breyer's Ice Cream Church of Phil?

If you're short on cash, you might want to combine your place of worship with another business, so you have something like Pete's House of Worship & Pancakes, or The Temple of Harzabian of the Carpet Cleaning Experts.

Affording Your House of Worship

Unless you chose the whole world as your shrine, one of the biggest expenses your religion will have is the cost of your house of worship. Getting the money together for a temple, church, shrine, etc., is no small feat. Here are a few examples of how other people made it happen.

Wristbands

If you have kids, or are a douchebag, you've paid for one of those little rubber wristbands that say things like LIVESTRONG or WWJD? They're surprisingly inexpensive to order in bulk and can be made to say all sorts of things, like: I KILL INFIDELS or INFERNAX SAVES or I'M GOD AND YOU'RE NOT, or . . . anything. Sell them for three times what you paid for them, and if they catch on at school or at the golf course, you can really do well. Try *www.24hourwristbands.com* or *www.motivators.com* for details on ordering your custom-made wristbands. (I make no guarantees about the quality of the product offered at these websites, nor do I receive a kickback for mentioning them, though that's a great idea for the next edition.)

Pancake Breakfast

Everybody likes pancakes, and they're inexpensive to make, especially if you use the cheapest ingredients possible (unless God/Goddess/Goat has instructed you to eat only organic vegan or only organic vegans). Go to Costco or Sam's Club (surely someone among your followers is a member; if not, you can always make it a condition of the next convert's admission to the congregation). Buy in bulk, then rope in the congregation as volunteer cooks and servers. If they burn the pancakes, that's just all a jovial part of being in fellowship with each other.

Everything you need, such as pots, pans, dishes, and so on can be rented, but be careful to watch every last penny of your expenses. You're shooting for bringing in three times what you spend. Advertising is essential, so get those flyers printed.

Chili Cook-off

Everybody who makes chili thinks theirs is the best chili in the world and many of them are willing to pay an entrance fee to serve it to your congregation to prove it. You can get money from the entrance fees and also charge people to come in and try all those great chilies, none of which is better than my chili, which rules over all chili.

Extortion

This is a great idea for more aggressive churches, biker death cults, survivalist collectives, and Scientologists. If you're sure you control the afterlife, eventually you'll want to control how people get there, so your threats will have some real *oomph*. A few high-profile hostages can net you enough money to hire the architect, at least. Of course, you can always just kidnap the architect.

Own Everything in the First Place

The ancient Egyptian pharaohs didn't have to suffer much over how to pay for the construction of their pyramids. For all intents and purposes, they owned Egypt itself and everything and everyone in it. I won't say that this is impossible to manage now, but if you try it in the United States, expect stiff competition from current owner Goldman Sachs.

Twinkies

The Harrisonville United Methodist Church in Harrisonville, Missouri, held a Deep Fried Twinkies Fundraiser, and you can, too. Again, buy in bulk from the warehouse clubs. To appeal to Twinkie purists, offer non-deep-fried versions as well. Sell the Twinkies for a 300 percent markup. You can also suggest that perhaps your God/Goddess/

Goat has taken all of the calories out of *these* Twinkies. People who love Twinkies will buy Twinkies, and will not care what they're supporting in the process.

Benefit Concerts

This is a particularly fun way to get celebrity spokespeople up in front of not only the faithful, but would-be converts, too. If your celebrity spokesperson isn't a musician, fear not; a movie or TV star can lead a prayer, introduce the band, and come on between songs to appeal for donations. You might be surprised how inexpensive some bands are to book—these will be bands that currently reside in the "where are they now" file, but can still bring in a paying crowd. I once saw Survivor at a suburban Chicago Fourth of July fireworks display and they were awesome. They played "Eye of the Tiger" twice!

Gummy Bears

Task the children of your congregation with going door-to-door selling gummy bears. These can be purchased in bulk cheaply, packaged in plastic bags with your religion's URL written on it, and sold for an extremely high markup. Only the most hardhearted individuals can refuse the entreaties of a sweet, gap-toothed child asking for their support. Those hardhearted individuals can later be targeted for re-education by your fanatics.

CHAPTER 13

Relax, It's a Holy Day

*or, work really hard,
it's a holy day*

A holy day is a day set aside for religious observance. Some people set aside Monday nights to pray to the gods of football, for example. You could choose every other Tuesday afternoon, or nights of the waxing gibbous moon, or February 29 for your regular worship/ritual/meetup. It's up to you. However, keep in mind that you will delight your followers by having special holy days in addition to the regular ones. You know Christmas? Like that. During these special holy days, which you might call High Holy Days or Holiest of Holy Days or Extra Special Holy Days or whatever sounds impressive, you'll want to kick it up a notch for your followers. You'll want to have special rituals or special rules that govern these days—and you can have different rules for different days. So, one holy day may require fasting whereas another may require feasting. This approach ensures that all of your followers will feel satisfied that their need for pain or pleasure is being attended to. Also, you can test people's devotion to your religion by giving them quizzes about the holy days.

It's probably best to start with one day and then add more as needed. Choose a day in which something significant in your religion happened: you were born, or the burning bush spoke to you, or the goat pledged his undying love, etc.

Holy Days 101

If you're too busy reining in your fanatics or mounting your inquisition to read the rest of this chapter, here is what you need to know in a nutshell: Some holy days are festive occasions, full of feasting and merrymaking, but others are somber affairs, even days that people really have to struggle to get through. Decide how many holy days there are, what their significance is, and what you expect to do on particular holy days. Keep holy days in mind while you're writing your scripture, and especially when you're creating your calendar (see Chapter 4).

Sample Holy Days (for Your Inspiration)

To give you inspiration, here are some sample holy days and explanations of how they're celebrated. Keep in mind your answer to the question in the Introduction quiz, "Holy days are best observed . . ."

January 14: Makar Sankranti

The first festival of the Hindu solar year celebrates the northward movement of the sun, and the lengthening of the days. It also marks the defeat of the demon Sankarasur by the deity Sankranti. Is there a demon in *your* scripture that was defeated on a certain day? If your holy book is unclear, you still have time to edit. Think about how that story might inform the ritual. It might be fun to, say, have a piñata in the shape of the demon or other monster that your congregation can beat on with a stick.

If you answered A, B, or C on the quiz, your religion will probably have a holy day similar in spirit to Makar Sankranti.

February 1: Imbolc

This feast in honor of the Celtic goddess Brigid is thought to be the precursor to our contemporary Groundhog Day. If you're creating a new religion now, it's hard to back-date your holy days in order to claim that something like Groundhog Day ripped you off. That being the case, you might want to try starting with Groundhog Day and building a new layer of religious significance around it. Make the groundhog something like a saint; for example, St. Shadowus, or Santa Bucktoothia.

It's way too cold in February to do anything naked, but Imbolc might have something to inspire people who answered anything but E on the quiz.

March 21: Nouruz

The Zoroastrian New Year's Day is based on a very old and confusing calendar, which just goes to show that the day the year begins is an arbitrary choice. Why does the year have to start in the dead of winter? I think starting the year in the spring makes more sense. Plants and animals are born in the spring, flourish in the summer of youth, go to seed in autumn, and get all cold and gray in winter, only to die and be reborn again in spring.

I'd imagine that anyone who answered C or F might like a nice spring rebirth.

April 17: The Feast of St. Wando

If you're Catholic and have never heard of this saint, let alone marked his feast day, shame on you, poser. Wando was a Benedictine monk from France, and that's pretty much all I know about him. This is a good example, though, of the perils of an over-crowded pantheon. Not that Catholics think St. Wando is a god, *per se*, but if you have too many gods, and all of them need their own holy days, feasts, festivals, or whatnot, it gets hard for people to keep track, and tends to dilute the importance of the major holy days.

Anyone who answered A and C on the quiz can't go wrong setting up a feast.

May (first full moon): Vesak

Buddha's birthday, also known as Visakah Puja or Buddha Day, is Buddhism's big holiday, celebrating not just the birth, but also the enlightenment, and subsequent death, of Buddha. Whether you worship one god or many, if that god wasn't truly eternal, with no beginning or end, the day that god was born is a pretty obvious holy day. Ordinary people celebrate their birthdays, so it only makes sense that you celebrate your god's, too. It might be fun to offer up sacrifices on your god(s)'s birthday(s)—like holy birthday presents.

This is a quiz triple threat: A, C, and E.

June 10: Day of Anahita

Anahita was a Persian goddess who eventually had an asteroid named after her. If you can get your deities' names to NASA, there's a pretty good chance that eventually some heavenly body will bear the name of a member of your pantheon. How cool would that be? The big Roman gods have already claimed the major planets, and it might not seem all that cool to have a mere asteroid named for your god, but just as tents can be replaced by churches, and churches are eventually overshadowed by cathedrals, if you play your cards right you might get your foot in the door with an asteroid and eventually have an as-yet-undiscovered planet named after your god. After all, eventually they're going to have to do something about Uranus.

This one is so obscure, it pretty much doesn't matter what you answered on the quiz.

July 9: Martyrdom of the Bab

A Bahá'í holy day, the Martyrdom of the Bab, commemorates the death of the Bab, who was executed by firing squad on July 9, 1850. This is one of those sad days. It's not a good thing when one of the founding fathers of your religion is killed, but working this sort of concept into the scripture early will help plant the seeds for a holy day in honor of your death. I know that when I die, I want everybody to take that day off from work every year to offer up prayers of apology. I told you I was sick, and you didn't believe me.

This might be the only holy day that people who answered either A or E might find inspirational.

August 23: Vulcanalia

A totally kick-ass sounding holiday on which the Romans threw living fish into fires as sacrifices to the volcano god Vulcan. If I were going to resurrect the worship of Vulcan, I would hold a huge, all-day heavy metal concert every August 23, culminating in celebrity worshiper Ozzy Osbourne biting the head off a live fish. Awesome!

Think seriously about something like Vulcanalia if you answered B or F on the quiz.

September 7: Philmas

Philites worldwide pause to celebrate Phil's birthday by Eating of His Chili and Reading of His Books.

You can celebrate Philmas regardless of your answer on the quiz. Philmas is for everyone!

October 31: Samhain

It's only called Samhain (pronounced Sow-een, just to confuse you) if you ask one of your Wiccan friends; it's Halloween if you ask one of your kids. This dark and cold autumn night traditionally commemorates people who have died, hence the whole creepy death theme. You can incorporate a holy day like this into your calendar, and celebrate it by DVRing a bunch of old horror movies from TCM. And eating candy.

If you answered A, C, or E on the quiz, you should find inspiration in Samhain.

November: Quecholli

This festive time is a great way for families to get together for ritual hunts and the bloody sacrifice of slaves in honor of the Aztec god Mixcoatl. If yours is one of those human-sacrificing religions, you might want to think about multiple holy days every year, each one set aside to sacrifice a different sort of person, such as slaves on Quecholli, gladiators on Tlacaxipehualiztli, or children on Huey Tozoztli.

Read up on Quecholli if you answered A or C on the quiz.

December 24: Demon Revels Da Meur

Screw Christmas Eve and your grandmother's lame-ass party. This Satanist holy day, also known as the High Grand Climax, is a day to sacrifice male infants, torture both men and women, have sex, probably get a tattoo or something, and listen to Marilyn Manson. Just think of it as achieving High Grand Satan Cred. Be advised, though, that if you celebrate this holiday, the FBI will probably put you on some sort of list.

This is a good one for you if you answered either A, E, or F on the quiz.

CHAPTER 14

Boot Your Sons and Daughters Out of the Nest

when it's time to grow up

Children are children and adults are adults, but frankly it can sometimes be hard to tell the difference. That's why you'll want to have an adulthood rite in your religion. This way, you'll know who's an adult and therefore can be held to adult standards (for example, signing over their life savings, tithing, etc.) and who is still a child and can reasonably be expected to believe everything you say.

The adulthood rite is especially useful if your dogma includes strict rules about when people can or cannot have sex, get married, procreate, and so on. Generally these experiences are only allowed for adults, which means that adolescents are already out there doing them, but don't let that discourage you. Insist that said adolescents participate in an adulthood rite before giving the official approval of sex/marriage/procreation. An adulthood rite can be a source of pride for everyone involved—it can also provide a tidy stream of revenue if you work it right.

Sample Adulthood Rites

Here are some sample adulthood rites to give you inspiration:

Drug the Kid

The Algonquin tribe of Quebec gave pubescent boys the wicked-strong hallucinogen wysoccan to blur their memories of childhood, ostensibly to clear their minds of trivial, childlike things to make room for all the important adult things they were going to have to remember. The drug was often way too effective, resulting in widespread memory loss so severe that the kids could no longer recognize their own families. This was sort of like jumping over adulthood entirely, and going from childhood to senility.

However, if you can find something like this drug it could be useful not only for getting kids to stop talking about Harry Potter but to erase an adult convert's memory of her previous religion.

Cow Jumping

This sounds like fun. The Hamar, in Ethiopia, when they think a boy is old enough, have him strip naked and jump over cows while the tribe cheers him on. You could have kids jump over all sorts of stuff that's more or less the size of a cow. Biker cults might like this one. Have the kid jump over a motorcycle, or jump over something else on a motorcycle. You get the picture. But unless you're a Penn State football coach, let's not do it naked.

Lock Her Up

In the ritual known as Festa das Mocas Novas, girls of the Tukuna people of the Amazon rainforest are placed in a small cell for from four to as many as twelve weeks after their first menstruation. This dark little box is meant to simulate the underworld. A girl's tribe mates, wearing demon masks, occasionally try to scare her. Eventually she's led out under the protection of her family and thrown a nice party.

If you choose a similar approach, be aware that locking up kids in contemporary America is going to get you in trouble, so make sure you don't get caught.

Here's Your Hat, What's Your Hurry?

The ancient Chinese Capping Ceremony probably went on for hours, like Asian ceremonies tend to do, but this is a pretty simple one that shouldn't get you into hot water. A young man, age twenty-ish, is formally fitted with a cap, or has his hair tied up in a bun, and is then given a congratulatory speech by an elder of his family, who also admonishes him to stop acting like a kid, and start behaving like an adult. This will give you an opportunity to design your own special hat.

Encourage Enjoyment

Among the Krobo ethnic group in Ghana, a girl approaching womanhood undergoes an initiation ceremony during which a ritual mother encourages her to set aside her childish ways, and instructs her in how to become a good wife and mother. This includes learning to cook and care for others. She is also taught how to enjoy a happy sex life, which has shocked and incensed missionaries for centuries.

Ease Them In

The U.S. legal system isn't the only authority to recognize that kids may need to transition to adulthood, rather than being thrown right in. Muslim boys and girls start fasting during Ramadan and as they get older, the number of days they're required to fast increases until they, like the other adults, fast for the entire month. This is not quite a formalized ceremony, but recognizes a gradual transition from childhood to adulthood.

Getting American kids to fast, or give up anything, for that matter, will be a challenge. Think about the expectations you have for your adult worshipers, and then sit down and form a schedule to introduce various rituals, ceremonies, and so on over the course of a few years.

Happy Graduation

If your religion has a private school system of some kind, you might want to take a cue from the Hindu Sanskar Samavartana. More like a graduation ceremony than an adulthood rite, this is meant to transition a child from his studies in Gurukul, a school for kids starting at no older than twelve, to a life as a "householder." The child requires the permission of his guru before he can enter the ashram, which might be considered a sort of spiritual university.

This is a particularly good idea if your religion has a really long and intense learning curve. If your worshipers have to memorize a lot of rituals, multiple gods, long and complex prayers, and so on, making it through that education and passing your version of the SAT certainly deserves a little pomp and circumstance.

God(s) Help Us

Want a really good example of what *not* to do? Look no further than the Mardudjara aborigines, who live around Lake Disappointment in Australia. Starting as young as age ten, boys are split into groups, called *yalburu*, and sent off on what has got to be the most fucked up adulthood rite I've ever heard of. Now, keep in mind that there is no anesthetic of any kind used before, during, or after any of what follows.

After undergoing some preparatory work, including getting his front tooth knocked out, the kid is subjected to a circumcision. But not just any circumcision. The kid is laid on his back and one of the adult men sits on his chest to hold him down, while another slices off his foreskin, and apparently in a nasty, violent way, not like a good *moyle*. The boy is then expected to eat his own foreskin, which they call "good meat," swallowing it whole without chewing it. Then they go hunting, kill something, and cover themselves in blood to symbolize rebirth.

After all that, and while the boy's pee-pee is still healing, one of his mother's brothers will give him a girl from the village to take care of. The boy is expected to hunt for her, and whatnot. There's certainly no hanky-panky going on. When he's finally healed, it's time for the grand finale.

The newly circumcised almost-man has the underside of his penis sliced open while he kneels over a fire so the blood can drip into the flames and be purified. Supposedly this is some kind of mock-menstruation done in honor of the women of the tribe.

Now, my son, you are a man. Sorry about your brutally mangled penis.

In contemporary American society, the legal system has dramatically watered down the transition from child to adult, slowly introducing certain elements of adulthood at various ages. You can get a driver's license when you're sixteen; buy pornography, vote, get a tattoo, or join the army when you're eighteen; buy alcohol when you're twenty-one; and rent a car when you're twenty-five.

Other cultures and religions provide for a more well-defined cut-off. But just as a thirteen-year-old Jewish boy who's had his Bar Mitzvah still can't buy beer, secular laws probably will not recognize your adulthood rite.

CHAPTER 15

I Now Pronounce You Husband(s) and/or Wive(s)

*and hurry, before they pass the
defense of marriage act*

Unless your religion espouses free love, you'll need some sort of mating ceremony to sort out who can have sex with whom, who can have children with whom, and so on. Though it may seem like none of your business, imagine what would happen if people just did whatever they wanted? That's why God/Goddess/Goat has got to get involved. Left to their own devices, people will almost certainly lead undisciplined, chaotic, and happy lives, which would be wrong.

A mating ceremony (also called a wedding ceremony or a marriage ritual) allows you to continue meddling in your followers' lives long after they've concluded their adulthood rite. You can also use it as a method for recruiting and retaining converts by forbidding followers from marrying outside the religion. If they can't marry a person of a different faith, then they won't be seduced by that faith and start giving their tithes elsewhere. Also, if someone wants to marry a person of a different religion, then that person will have to convert to your religion before you approve. Brilliant, eh? The conversion can come with a fee and a ceremony of its own.

What Marriage Is

Before you can decide what type of mating ceremony you'll have, you first have to decide what marriage *is*—at least according to your religious principles.

Let's start with how you answered that quiz in the Introduction. Finish this sentence: Marriage is . . .

A Loving Union Between Two or More Consenting Adults

A lot of the secular world is moving toward this idea, which recognizes various alternative lifestyles but prevents slavery and child abuse. Both of those words, "consenting" and "adult," are of equal importance.

The more permissive you are, though, the more likely you are to bump up against various secular laws. Polygamy is illegal, and in many states so is same-sex marriage. If you want to try to change those laws, you'll be putting your religion, and your followers, on the front lines of a particularly catty battle between highly entrenched ideologues. Of course, you're starting your own religion, so just start off being a highly entrenched ideologue and you'll be ready for the fight from the get-go.

A Loving Union Between a Man and a Woman

This is the traditional approach, and it's kind of the easy way out, but will keep your religion from being too controversial, at least on that front, and marriage rights is a hot-button topic right now.

It's estimated that about 10 percent of the population is gay, so if you ban gay marriage you'll have to be prepared for one out of ten people in your community (not counting the straight people who support gay rights) to avoid your religion just as they're forced to avoid others. You might be able to balance this, though, if 10 percent of the people in your town are raging homophobes.

This is a good option for religions that want to fly under the radar, and slip into town without ruffling any feathers.

A Loving Union Between a Man and Several Women

This approach, often favored by Mormon fundamentalists, some Muslims, and many Senegalese, can certainly appeal to male converts who like to believe they are doing the will of God/Goddess/Goat.

However, before you allow for polygamy in your religion, think about whether or not that's really sustainable, if, say, the wealthiest 1 percent of men are married to 99 percent of the women. The response to that will not be as half-hearted as Occupy Wall Street, believe me.

A Loving Union Between a Woman and Several Men

This is the sort of marriage currently only practiced among the Porn People of California's San Fernando Valley, though it may be perfect for similar matriarchal religions in which women are revered as goddesses. The downside to this approach is that you may not have enough men in your religion for each woman to have several partners, meaning some women may feel left out. However, if you do some recruiting among recent divorcées, this becomes less of a problem. They will be more interested in sacrificing the men than in sleeping with them. That creates a different problem, but no one said starting a religion was easy.

A Loving Union Between Me and All of the Men/Women in the Church

Best left to those cults in which you have set yourself up as God, Goddess, or something like a god. It is the twenty-first century after all, so feel free to mix and match genders as you see fit. The benefits to this arrangement are obvious, but it can be exhausting trying to keep everyone happy, or at least not throwing things at you, so try to limit the number of your spouses to fewer than one hundred.

Banned

Who says your religion has to recognize marriage at all? Think about banning marriage, if not mating, outright, or simply ignoring it. This works best if your religion falls on either far end of the spectrum: (a) hippy-dippy peace and love or (b) hardcore death cult. If you're certain that the world is going to end next Thursday, for instance, what's the point of all that wedding planning and expense? Likewise, if you're going to live forever in a state of existential bliss, promising to be with someone until death do you part has no meaning, because death will never part you—and let's be honest, a lifelong commitment is too much for a lot of people. Stretch that out to eternity and you'll just end up with a bunch of single people anyway.

Traditional Wedding Gifts

You can't come to a wedding empty-handed, and what you bring can say a lot about you, the bride and groom, your family, and theirs ... or how devout a follower of your shared religion you are. Set aside secular staples, such as toasters and fondue sets, and create a set of traditional wedding gifts for your own religion. Here are a few ideas:

Twinkies: Everyone loves Twinkies and they're cheap, but then it's the thought that counts. And if you have enough Twinkies you don't have to buy an expensive wedding cake.

Silver things: This traditional gift among the Hindu faithful symbolizes a prosperous future for the newlyweds. Take this a step beyond your grandmother's never-used silverware and make it specific: a silver candy dish full of Holy Gummy Bears?

Trashy lingerie: Hey, we all know what this whole to-do is leading up to, why not help make it sizzle?

Sacrifices: Sometimes, gifts are made to the deities themselves, leaving the betrothed to fend for themselves. Traditional Mayan wedding ceremonies include sacrificial offerings of rice, fruit, corn, and beans. You tailor the offerings to your religion: used motor oil for the Brotherhood of the Gearheads, last year's wardrobe for the Sisterhood of the Perpetually Well-Dressed.

The Marriage Ritual

Once you've decided what marriage means for your religion, you need to determine what the ritual will look like. Regardless of who's marrying whom, most people come for the ritual, the ceremony, the sense of community and shared expression of love, and the presents.

Here's a handy list of elements you'll want to think about including in your marriage ritual:

Vows

The default wedding vows you tend to see on TV sitcoms come from the Anglican Book of Common Prayer. You know the one:

I, (state your name), take thee, (state the other person's name), to be my wedded (husband/wife) to have and to hold from this day forward, for better or for worse, for richer or poorer, in sickness or in health, to love and to cherish, till death do us part.

There are practically limitless variations on that basic theme of "from now on, we're in this together." Technically, vows are spoken by the people getting married, but feel free to mix it up, and however nicely, impose marriage from the pulpit, as in the Blessing of the Apaches:

Now you will feel no rain, for each of you will be shelter for the other.

Now you will feel no cold, for each of you will be warmth to the other.

Now there will be no loneliness, for each of you will be companion to the other.

Now you are two persons, but there is only one life before you.

May beauty surround you both in the journey ahead and through all the years.

May happiness be your companion and your days together be good and long upon the earth.

Dress Code

Traditional western weddings have defaulted to the elaborate white gown for the bride and formal black tuxedo for the groom, but this is your religion, so don't feel as though you have to be bound by that tradition. The white wedding dress is a relatively recent concept, apparently popularized by Queen Victoria in 1840. In Hindu weddings, the idea of the bride wearing white, a color reserved for funerals, is utterly terrifying. Hindu brides show up for their wedding ceremonies draped in the brightest shades of red, orange, and yellow they can find, which lends a more celebratory, less somber effect to the whole affair.

When determining the groom's attire, consider that very few men like to wear tuxedos, which are heavy, hot, and constraining. And because so few men actually own tuxedos, a groom will probably end up renting one, and that's just weird.

This is your religion, so you get to choose the colors, fabrics, and so on. You might want the bride and groom to appear naked: going into their marriage the way they came into the world, as though their lives are starting over fresh. You may have traditional robes, hats, cowled cloaks, togas . . . you tell me.

Shotguns

In the traditional shotgun wedding, the bride is required to be pregnant, and the farther along the better. The groom is required to not want to be there, and more so than is normal with grooms. The father of the bride traditionally holds the shotgun, covering the reluctant groom until that no-account hayseed makes an honest woman out of his little girl.

I'm not sure the shotgun wedding is anything but a piece of American folklore, but that doesn't mean your religion can't make it a reality. After all, UFOs dropping A-bombs into volcanoes was just a science fiction story until Scientology came along.

Drinks

In Japanese Buddhist wedding ceremonies the bride and groom perform a little ritual called *San-sankudo no Sakazuki,* which means "three, three, nine times." Starting with the smallest of three special cups called *sakazuki,* the bride and groom each take three sips of sake from each cup.

The number three is significant to Buddhists, but by all means feel free to change the number and size of the cups. If your religion isn't keen on alcohol, sub in juice or water. If you're a little more gung ho, you can use a stronger liquor, human blood, or other liquids that will more severely test the mettle of the betrothed.

Symbol of Unity

In western cultures, exchanging rings is often part of the ceremony and doing so gives a concrete symbol to the union. A ring can serve as a reminder of one's marriage, in case one tends to forget in the presence of alcohol. It is also a discreet "hands off" sign (or in some cases, the opposite). You can substitute other talismans, if you wish, such as a pretty stone or a Ferrari. Additionally, you can have the couple/group/crowd perform an act of unity, such as lighting one large single candle from a group of little ones (one little candle for each person in the union), or high-fiving each other, etc.

CHAPTER 16

Cast Out the faithless

when only excommunication will do

Though the word "excommunication" has decidedly Catholic roots—basically, it means you are banned from the community ("communion") of believers—it's come to describe any process under which anyone is tossed out of any religion.

As your new religion grows and you attract more followers, eventually you're going to find some troublemakers among the faithful. Does your holy book or epic poem have a clear set of guidelines for how devotees are expected to behave? The more rigid your rules, the more likely it is that someone is going to break them. So even as you set those rules, you should be thinking about various forms of penance and discipline, up to and including kicking the heretic out.

Penance and Discipline

When a follower breaks a minor rule (missing a service, leering at someone else's spouse, parking in your spot) you must decide how the infraction is to be treated. In most religions, the goal is to make the sinner feel remorse for his/her misdeeds, in order to correct the behavior and make sure that it won't be repeated. Although you may not believe in the perfectibility of people, you can teach them to avoid pain. There's nothing like a hefty fine to ensure feelings of regret.

Other options include:

- Public shaming. In unison, the entire congregation can wag their fingers at the culprit while saying, "Tsk, tsk!"
- Prayer. You can pray for the miscreant, make the miscreant pray, or both.
- Temporary exclusion. This is the adult version of the time-out.
- Act of humiliation. You can require the miscreant to do something really embarrassing, such as wearing a sandwich board listing his/her sins while walking on the busiest sidewalk in town.

Expulsion of the Heretics

If followers commit more egregious acts, you'll need to consider expelling them from the congregation. What constitutes "more egregious acts"? The answer is in how you responded to the quiz in the Introduction. Someone must be immediately excommunicated if he or she . . .

Harshes the Group's Mellow

As anyone who has experienced a really pleasant moment of existential enlightenment knows, nothing is more detrimental to such spiritual growth as the person who spoils it all by demanding that you get off your ass and go to school/work/your own house. Therefore, you can let it be written that people who do that will be excommunicated. However, the drawback to this approach is that practically everybody has harshed someone else's mellow a time or two, and soon you'll be left with no followers. If you decide to use this approach, consider a three-strikes-and-you're-out rule, which gives everyone a little leeway if they haven't had their morning coffee.

Commits a Mortal Sin

This approach works best for those religions that have a lot of dogma and high expectations for personal behavior. You will need to give your devotees a very clear list of exactly what these sins are that will get you kicked out. Think of it in terms of the workplace. You'll expect to get fired from your job at the gas station if you steal from the register, but if you show up ten minutes late, maybe you'll just get a written warning. Mortal sins tend to coincide with secular laws. It's against the law to embezzle from your employer, but there is no law against getting stuck in traffic or waking up late, or even just being lazy and disorganized. On the other hand, it's your religion, so if you think being lazy and disorganized is a mortal sin, then by all means list it as such and excommunicate anyone who fails your filing exam.

However, be aware that if you make too many human tendencies into mortal sins, you can create more problems than you solve. For example, if you make masturbation a mortal sin you'll end up with parishioners who just lie to you as much as two or three times a day depending on their ages and situations, or within a few months you'll have excommunicated everybody. In this case, maybe just a quick hand-washing ritual will do.

Fails to Adequately Tithe

Not that you're only in it for the money or anything, but the Resplendent Pagoda of the Stars is not going to build itself. Going back to the workplace example, it's not at all unusual for certain occupations, such as sales associates, to have a set minimum sales figure per month, quarter, or year. If you don't make your quota, out you go. Once you've determined the amount of money you expect from your faithful, it's okay to hold their feet to the fire (in some cases literally, if you're on the evil death cult end of the spectrum).

Clear and reasonable expectations are, again, key. If you expect people to give you *all* of their money, you'll have to make sure you're taking care of at least their basic needs. The more pressure you put on people to stop spending money on anything but your temple's goals, the more likely they are to skim the tithe.

If you're only asking for a percentage of each follower's income, you still may want to set up a hardship clause. People experience setbacks: They get laid off, or have unexpected car repairs. If you're too strident, as with your frequent masturbators, you can find yourself excommunicating so many people you end up with no income at all.

Won't Have Sex with Me

If you're running one of those everybody-has-sex-with-you cults, then there's really no point in keeping people around who aren't having sex with you. This would be like employing someone to clean your house who just sits there and watches TV.

Keep in mind that it isn't technically sexual harassment if you tell them up front that if they come to you for spiritual guidance they will be expected to sleep with you. If they still join up . . . dude, awesome.

Refuses to Eat of the Flesh of the Unworthy

How does someone join a religion called Our Lady of Eating Human Flesh, then not show up for the annual sacrificial rite and barbecue? At this point, you're going to have to insist that the reluctant parishioner take a bite of Jim, here, or you may have to question his/her commitment to the Grail Movement.

Even if your religion doesn't practice cannibalism, this is a good example of excommunication as a result of ignoring or refusing your religion's primary sacrament. The same could be said for the Hugs 'N' Kisses Kult, for instance, if you have members who flatly refuse to either hug or kiss people—but maybe they only deserve full-on excommunication if they refuse to both hug *and* kiss people.

Farts During the Holiest of Holy Ceremonies
Self-explanatory.

Church and State

In 1981, a woman named Marian Guinn was accused of adultery by the Church of Christ of Collinsville, Oklahoma. Apparently she didn't think she'd done anything wrong, and would not repent her sins. Just before the church could formally excommunicate her, she withdrew her membership. But then the church elders went ahead and announced her excommunication to the flock. They took the further step of notifying other churches in the area of her sins.

Ms. Guinn, embarrassed by all this public talk of her naughty habits, filed a lawsuit against the church and its elders for the intentional infliction of emotional distress (calling her an adulterer made her feel bad about herself), and invasion of privacy (telling everybody she was an adulterer made everyone else feel bad about her).

The judge found in favor of the sinner, and awarded Ms. Guinn more than $400,000 in damages, based on the actions the church elders took after Ms. Guinn formally left the church.

This teaches us all: either excommunicate sinners fast, before they can quit, or stop talking about them the second they do quit.

After Expulsion

You should also consider what happens to heretics *after* they're excommunicated.

Obviously, excommunicated individuals are no longer welcome at the temple for prayers, sacrifices, and so on. Don't let their families bury the excommunicated in the temple catacombs. Don't let them keep bringing their kids to your daycare center. And they definitely lose their security deposits.

But these earthly chastisements aren't always enough.

The Ahl-i Haqq believe that if you commit grievous enough sins, not only are you to be excommunicated from the world community, but when you die you will be reincarnated as a dog, or other filthy, lowly animal. This transformation, known as metempsychosis, signifies how far the sinner has sunk in the eyes of God. A sub-sect of the Ahl-i Haqq, the Thoumaris, believe that these reincarnations can go on and on, with the sinner dying as a dog only to be reincarnated as another dog, as many as a million times. His soul is cleansed a little more each time until he can finally rejoin the sect as a human and once again enjoy God's good graces.

Take a lesson from this. If you assume a dog lives, say, ten years, you won't have to welcome the excommunicated sinner back into your fold for another ten million years after he or she dies. Problem solved on your end.

CHAPTER 17

Accept Burnt Offerings... or Not

sometimes, you just have to sacrifice something . . . or someone

Many religions include sacrifices, which are offerings meant to appeal to (or appease) God/Goddess/Goat for one reason or another, some of them ridiculous to outsiders but not to true believers. Basically, you are exchanging something (the sacrificial item) in order to get something back: God's favor, the spring rains, or your lost wallet.

If you decide to include sacrifice in your ritual, you can choose from among three different types: the sacrifice of material objects, animal sacrifice, and human sacrifice. Of these three, one is (within the general bounds of reason) perfectly legal in the United States, one is kind of in a gray area, and one will land you in jail for a very long time. Just sayin'.

Understanding the Three Types of Sacrifice

Before you decide which type of sacrifice is appropriate for your religion (or if you even want to use any type of sacrifice at all), you need to understand what each type entails. That way, when the burning bush speaks to you next Friday after happy hour at Texas Tex's, you can marshal a cogent argument about why you will or will not agree to pass along the bush's demands to your followers.

The Sacrifice of Material Objects

Sacrificing inanimate objects is generally a harmless ritual, so long as you do it in a safe way and the objects belong to you. Asking people to write down their sins, or their hopes and dreams, on a little piece of paper and then burning it, for example, is a nice approach to sacrifice, and not too scary for anyone. You can burn other things, too, like books you disagree with, that bill from the IRS, or pretty much whatever strikes your fancy, but remember not to burn buildings—that's arson, religion or no.

Burning things tends to destroy them completely, which is important in a sacrificial rite. If you just set something of value on the ground and chant over it for a few minutes, then take it back, it doesn't count as a sacrifice. Burying things, or throwing things in the ocean or a lake or river, works, too, and can be safer.

Archaeologists are pretty happy with certain cultures' propensity to sacrifice objects by burying them in the ground, which has the effect of preserving said objects for future study. In England, 2,000 years ago, it was common to sacrifice broken household objects by burying them, but don't be surprised if your god turns his nose up at your broken pot.

And archaeologists are getting increasingly creative, and well-funded, in their efforts to reclaim someone's material sacrifices. Even if you throw something into the deepest part of the ocean, somebody with letters after her name will eventually rent a submarine and retrieve it. However, you can be content with the fact that whatever it is you threw in there, or buried, is lost *to you*, so the sacrifice has been made.

In almost every case other than the Broken Pickle Jar People of Ancient Britain, devotees are asked to sacrifice something of value in hopes of appeasing greedy and judgmental gods. A number of Native American tribes, for instance, sacrificed corn or cornmeal. The Pawnee sacrificed corn mush, and the Iroquois offered up edibles such as beans and sunflower seeds. That may not seem like much to us, but in that time and place, these were the community's most valuable items.

By definition, a sacrifice has to be something it hurts you—at least a little—to lose. To that end you can ask your followers to sacrifice money. If you do, you should construct a hierarchy of expectations for this one. If you burn a $1 bill you only get a dollar's worth of grace, but a C-note buys forgiveness of practically all your sins. Most religious leaders would prefer you *donate* money rather than burn it, but to each his own. Another potential material sacrifice is the cell phone. If you can get a teenage girl to throw her cell phone in the font, you know you've got her for good. Don't have people bury their cell phones, though, or throw them in the ocean, as they contain toxic chemicals. Come to think of it, you might want to avoid inhaling the smoke from the sacrificial pyre of cell phones as well. And if you feel you may have to get in touch with your followers from time to time, you may want to pass on this one.

Animal Sacrifice

There aren't a lot of extant religions that still practice animal sacrifices, but in one landmark case the United States Supreme Court decided in favor of animal sacrifice . . . sort of. In the 1993 decision on *Church of Lukumi Babalu Aye v. City of Hialeah*, in which a Florida Santerían church was cited for performing animal sacrifices, the Court upheld the church's rights under the First Amendment.

This means that you may be able to incorporate animal sacrifice into your rituals without getting hauled into court, but you may also draw the wrath of PETA, and in a battle between PETA and your God/ Goddess/Goat, we wouldn't want to bet the farm on the outcome.

Bear in mind that if you choose to have an animal sacrifice as part of your ritual, you'll still have to follow the laws of your locale. You can't steal animals or hunt out of season, for example. Also, torturing the animals is frowned upon, and unless you're Michael Vick, may result in serious repercussions.

And then there's this to consider: Certain animals may not take too kindly to being sacrificed, and may try to bite you, leading to sepsis and other infections. Before you begin your animal sacrifice, maybe sedate the animal in question, or at least make sure your tetanus shots are up to date. The actual sacrifice can be a good job for a deacon or acolyte to do, while you watch from a safe distance.

One main drawback to including animal sacrifice in your ritual is that many people love animals, or say they do, and will be repelled by your religion instead of attracted to it. Host a nice barbecue instead.

Human Sacrifice

Human sacrifice has a long and rich history that has, for better or worse, tapered off. The Aztecs and other pre-Columbian people are perhaps the best known for their bloody rituals of human sacrifice that included the ritual eating of the dead. They tended to use human sacrifice in their big, gory temples to establish a constant level of shock and awe amongst the peasantry. This is one of the advantages of human sacrifice: It cows people into submission with the threat that they could be next. (The whole economic meltdown could have been avoided with a little judicious culling of bankers, for example.)

However, if you build a temple soaked in blood and entrails in most parts of the United States, the neighbors will eventually complain, probably with really passive-aggressive e-mails to the homeowners' association. And you do *not* want those people on your back.

At least when your religion is just starting out, avoid selecting sacrificial subjects from among your worshipers. If your people start to get the feeling that maybe they're next in line, they might not stick around until their number's up. And it can have a real dampening effect on recruitment, if word gets out that there's even a small chance that they'll at some point be shown their still-beating hearts, even as the rest of the flock begins to feed.

Don't Try This at Home

On December 6, 1987, Carl Junction, Missouri, teenagers Jim Hardy, Pete Roland, and Ron Clements bludgeoned fellow "Satanist" Steve Newberry to death while chanting "Sacrifice to Satan! Sacrifice to Satan!" This very likely reduced the total number of Satanists in Carl Junction, Missouri, by 25 percent.

All three of the surviving Carl Junction Satanists are now serving life sentences. Church and state are no longer separate on that count. A human sacrifice is murder, plain and simple, in every state in the union.

Virgin Sacrifice

But wait—there's more. Let's call this a bonus sacrifice. Like cornmeal, bits of pottery, or your neighbor's cat, we sacrifice that which has value to us, and who doesn't value a nice, comely virgin lass most of all?

If you commit to a program of virgin sacrifice, you're in for a difficult road. This practice never really caught on except in men's adventure magazines of the 1950s. Aside from all that stuff about capital murder and suchlike, the big problem with virgin sacrifice is finding a virgin in the first place.

If your church is located someplace like New Jersey, California, or within a fifty-mile radius of an amusement park or drive-in movie theater, virgin girls over the age of, say, thirteen are thin on the ground. Virgin sacrifice is best left to churches located in certain parts of the Middle East; some of the state of Idaho, except the areas immediately surrounding Boise or Coeur d'Alene; the city of Wheaton, Illinois; and the entire state of Utah.

An alternative is to have a virgin sacrifice her virginity, which a surprising number of virgins are quite willing to do, especially in the name of God/Goddess/Goat.

CHAPTER 18

Sample Religion 3: The Cult of the Blue Öyster

one hard rockin' evil biker death cult

The Cult of the Blue Öyster was founded by someone who answered mostly F on the quiz in the Introduction. The religion is based on the teachings of the great prophet Buck Dharma, whose holy song "(Don't Fear) the Reaper" comprises the entirety of the cult's scripture.

The cult meets every Friday after work at Betty's Bar & Grill out on Route 17, at least until they raise enough money to build their stepped pyramid decorated with the blood of sacrificial virgins, and kick-ass Metallica posters. They should be able to begin construction within the year, because the crystal meth they've been selling, cooked by the cult's Lord High Alchemist Pete "College Boy" Dickson, has been selling like crazy. It's been doing even better since last month when they sacrificed the county's last secular meth dealer out behind the Getty Avenue Projects. Crystal meth is not just the cult's primary source of income, but their holy sacrament as well.

The Cult of the Blue Öyster's holiest days are the six days beginning on Lemmas, December 24th, and ending with the Feast of Harley on the 29th. Lemmas celebrates the birthday of Lemmy Kilmister, frontman of the band Motörhead. Though their scripture is not based on a Motörhead song, the cult marks this day because Motörhead rocks and also because of the religious significance of the o-umlaut in both bands' names. Cultists are expected to start getting drunk at the turn of midnight on Lemmas Eve and stay both awake (the sacramental meth helps) and drunk until noon on the Feast of Harley, which commemorates the birth of William Sylvester Harley, cofounder of the Harley-Davidson Motor Company.

They're also expected to attend any Blue Öyster Cult comeback concert, and volunteer to act as security.

Children are not allowed to join the Cult of the Blue Öyster, which is open only to adult men and their bitches. When one of the sons of a current cult member turns sixteen he's brought by his father to a ceremony known as the Last Time You Do Anything for the Man.

First, the boy is taken to get his driver's license, with motorcycle endorsement. Once he has passed that test, he has done the last thing he will ever do for the Man. He is then made to drink beer until he vomits. Next he is sent to a motel room where he is met by a prostitute from the village, paid for by his father's closest living adult male relative. The next morning, he's in.

As for the daughter of a current cult member you better keep your goddamn hands off her, goddamn it—she is *not* going to end up like her mother if I have anything to say about it.

But it's the marriage ceremony of the Blue Öyster Cultists that's the most sweet and heartfelt. When a cultist finds a bitch he can stand for more than a couple of days, he brings her to the annual Sturgis Motorcycle Rally where, in full view of the rest of the cult, he falls to one knee and recites the first three lines of the most holy hymn, "(Don't Fear) the Reaper."

If the woman is receptive to his advances, she replies with the next line. If she isn't, she hits him over the head with a half-empty bottle of Jack. A brawl then breaks out between his peeps and hers, which continues until someone pulls a gun. Then cooler heads prevail and the combatants buy each other drinks and get on with their lives.

If encouraged to continue, the would-be groom beckons his baby to come on, and she responds with the title of the sacred hymn. They continue in this fashion, trading lines of the song, until the gentleman finally identifies himself as the bride's man. Then they're engaged and everyone gets really wasted.

A year later, the couple returns to Sturgis for the wedding ceremony, and again standing before the assembled cultists, they speak the rest of the holy words.

The groom is hidden behind a curtain and, when the bride is ready, the entire congregation chants the second verse of the sacred hymn. When commanded to do so by the holy words, the groom throws back the curtain, embraces his betrothed, and cautions her not to be afraid, and beckons her to come on.

The bride responds in the third person that she isn't afraid, and so on, again trading line for line until the sacred hymn is completed.

Then the drinking really begins.

Though the cultists of the Blue Öyster are often violent, including with each other, they maintain a strict code of honor. Once a member of the cult, always a member of the cult, and if any follower is threatened, all followers are threatened.

There are several active cult groups in the prison systems of both the United States and Canada, where they continue to spread the holy sacrament to anybody with a couple of bucks or a carton of smokes.

Life: So You Can Interfere with It

Religions can explain all sorts of things, like how the world was created and when, why the sky is blue, and what happens to us after we die. But science does a much better job explaining all those things, so you need to have something else to offer potential converts. Fortunately, what many people want from religion is an instruction book for how to live their lives and to be told what is right and what is wrong, because it can be very confusing to try to figure it out for themselves. This is where you come in. You have opinions about how people should live their lives, don't you? (If you don't, possibly you are not cut out for starting your own religion, and may want to reconsider this career path.) This step will teach you how to collect those opinions and put them to good use in your religion.

CHAPTER 19

Abstinence Only— Unless Otherwise Instructed

sex is dirty and sinful, unless you're being fruitful and multiplying

The mating ritual (marriage, wedding ceremony, etc.) is just one way religions attempt to control the sexual impulses, habits, and proclivities of their followers. However, marriage, on its own, rarely constrains the sexual impulse completely and you will need to develop other methods of keeping unruly libidos in line. This is where religion is far superior to science: Science will just tell you that careless sex with lots of partners can lead to deadly diseases, whereas religion can tell you that careless sex with lots of partners can lead to hell and the eternal damnation of your immortal soul!

Or, if you want to *encourage* careless sex, your religion can position it as the gateway to redemption and spiritual awakening, but this is not a popular approach, as people generally want to believe that anything that feels so good must be bad for them and the badder it is, the more they like it.

As you develop your own new religion, you'll want to put some serious thought into the subject, even if it makes you uncomfortable . . . no, *especially* if it makes you uncomfortable to think about it. One of the most compelling reasons to start your own religion is to teach people to think and behave like you do, so if sex makes you uneasy, you'll want your devotees to share that discomfort.

Determining What Your Religion Teaches about Sex

You will need to think about what you want your followers to do about their sexual impulses, because they will have them and they will expect you to cough up some rules for them to follow. That is to say, you need to find out what God/Goddess/Goat wants your followers to do about their sexual impulses.

Start by looking at your answer to the quiz in the Introduction. You were asked to complete the sentence: Sex is to be enjoyed . . .

Between Loving, Consenting Adults

In this approach, if two people (consenting and adult) get that lovin' feeling, well, then, who are you to interfere? This is a sane and sensible approach, which means most religions won't tolerate it.

If you want to be more involved in your followers' sex lives, or if you think it's just plain wrong to enjoy sex, this approach will prove unsatisfactory to you and you'll want to choose another.

Between an Adult Man and an Adult Woman Who Love Each Other, or Have Had One Too Many Appletinis

If you're trying to appeal to the greatest number of followers, this is probably the most useful approach for you to take. People feel better about careless sex if they can blame it on love or intoxication and would prefer you not condemn their immortal souls because of a particularly raucous happy hour. Could they help it if they felt reckless just this once? Also, most people are conformists and don't want to think about doing anything out of the mainstream. Thus, endorsing the mainstream approach will win you many converts, if you're looking for mainstream converts.

However, if you're slightly more open-minded, or if your God/Goddess/Goat is, then this approach may be less appealing. Women who want to get it on with women (and men *vis-à-vis* men) are excluded from this approach, as are people who enjoy group sex or who swing both ways. If you make them feel too bad about themselves, they will probably not want to join your religion.

Pass the Plate

Consider that one way to diversify your revenue streams is to grant dispensations to people who want to have sex outside your religion's accepted parameters. Thus, you can have a fairly rigorous interpretation of who can have sex when and with whom, but not really enforce it. That way, people can come to you and admit they had sex with three men and a dog and they'll be forgiven if they pay a stated fine. It's helpful to have a price list of the cost of various dispensations so that people can decide what they can afford ahead of time.

Within the Confines of Marriage

This is an excellent approach for many religions. Because everyone wants to have sex, if you say that it is only sanctioned within a marriage, then everyone will want to get married so they can have sex without going to hell or whatever deeply disappointing consequence would otherwise result. So (and here's the genius), you charge a small fee for the marriage rite and you get to (a) control people's sex lives and (b) make a little money on it.

The trick is to get people married fast enough, at a young enough age, to compete with the primal physical urge to mate. Otherwise they'll be having sex outside of marriage no matter what you say about it. If you get enough kids racing off to the altar, ban birth control, and leave them to their natural urges once the wedding reception is over, you should hear the pitter-patter of little cultists in no time.

The easier you make it to get divorced, too, the better, allowing followers to cycle through. Don't underestimate the value of multiple marriages to the church coffers. Charge a reasonable fee for both divorce and marriage and you can set up a nice repeat business to keep you in candles and Amy Grant CDs for years to come.

In Some Extremely Specific Way

What better way to control your followers' sexual impulses than to be really controlling? Maybe they can only have sex after getting permission from you (with ten days' notice and the payment of a small endorsement fee). Maybe they can have sex with anyone but only on every other full moon. If you choose this approach, try to have a reason why: Griselda the Great's headache only subsided six times a year and we celebrate by having sex on those six days, or some such explanation.

During the Monthly Fornication Rite

The ritual sex orgy can be very appealing, especially if you like sex but don't have a particular impulse toward monogamy. Though your religion is entirely new, your converts will be coming from a largely monogamous society and so they probably won't have much experience with sex orgies, polyamory, or even performing in public. Even though people (mostly young men) will make a beeline to your religion if you promise them orgies, it won't be long before someone gets his or her feelings hurt. Expect fights to break out, couples to pair off, and sex rites that end up with fifty straight guys playing video games and getting drunk because no women showed up. In most of the civilized world this religion is known as "College."

Constantly

Unless you establish Viagra as a holy sacrament this approach might be a little difficult for your male converts, but is certainly worth a try. Asking your followers to engage in sex constantly requires you to enter into full-scale cult mode. You'll need everyone to live together in as self-sufficient a temple or compound as possible. After all, people can't have sex while doing the grocery shopping, nor can they have sex all day at work. Even the most progressive companies may find this creates a hostile work environment, though you might be able to get away with it at larger, more risk-averse corporations who operate under stricter regulations and are afraid of one religious discrimination lawsuit breeding more and more just like it.

Environment and Sexual Morality

Atheist scholar Richard Dawkins thinks a religion's sexual hang-ups have something to do with environment. He asserts that desert people end up with religions that have strict rules against nudity, which are not found among tropical people. Wearing clothes all the time makes sense when you live in a place where the sun can actually roast you alive in the daytime and it gets down to freezing at night. Judaism, Christianity, and Islam all come out of the deserts of the Middle East, and they all tend to be "keep your clothes on" faiths. But people from tropical environments, India or Polynesia for instance, can walk around naked pretty much year round, and this, apparently, ends up with them having more sex.

CHAPTER 20

Education: The Great Evil

except if you attend one of our expensive private schools

Now that your followers are having officially sanctioned sex, which results in babies who are new followers, you have to make sure those babies are brought up right. It's never too early for your religion to begin interfering with—I mean, *enriching*—the lives of your devotees, so you'll need to consider the education of your youngest followers.

There are, traditionally, two different kinds of education. In a public (or secular) education, religion is at least de-emphasized if not entirely eliminated from the school day. Then there's parochial (or religious) schooling, which is either an addition to public school (such as Sunday School or Hebrew School) or replaces public school entirely so that the religious institution takes on the full responsibility for a child's education.

Education Considerations

If you think that providing a parochial school education is the best approach for your followers' children, you'll want to consider that many children who attend parochial school actually leave the religion. That's cold, man. Here are some reasons why parochial schools fail:

Teachers Aren't Prepared for Inquisitive Kids

Any parent will tell you that the first word every baby learns to say is "mine," and the second word a baby learns to say is "why?" As a religious leader, you had better be ready for an awful lot of sentences that begin with words like "why," "how," and "when?"

The late George Carlin, a vocal atheist himself, talked about his own Catholic school upbringing, including this smartass question asked of a nun: "If God is all-powerful, can he build a rock so big and so heavy that even he, himself, can't lift it?" If you're starting with God as all-powerful creator of the universe, you'll have to really do some thinking to get past this, and make sure your teachers are ready with a plausible answer. Otherwise, the students will think you're full of shit, which doesn't induce loyalty.

Avoiding Common Education Traps

If you're starting fresh with a polytheistic pantheon, you can avoid the trap of not having an answer to the questions any reasonably bright eight-year-old will ask about your religion by making sure there is no "all-powerful" god. The God of the Earth *can* build a rock too heavy for the God of Strength to lift, until the God of Strength rises to the challenge and improves his strength until he can lift it, forcing the God of the Earth to build an even heavier rock. This can become a parable to encourage working hard to constantly improve yourself. This could also serve as a creation story for your religion—that ever-bigger, ever-heavier rock became the Earth itself, and when the God of Strength finally couldn't lift it, only then did all the gods of the pantheon know it was special enough to be populated with us, and everything else. (See? It's not that hard to come up with your own religion.)

The Teachers and Administrators Are Too Mean

Kids who are brought up in an environment of fear and abuse learn either to be afraid or to be abusers. Unless those are the values you wish your religion to impart, train your teachers to be reasonable, caring people. If your school is a happy place where kids feel safe, they'll be much more open to the rest of your religious teachings.

Your Religion Isn't the Most Compelling Reason to Go

When my wife was a little girl she went to an evangelical summer camp with one of her friends, even though my wife was raised a Catholic. After the first day she realized that the kids who raised their hands when the congregation was asked, "Have you been saved?" not only got a piece of candy but got to leave church and go swimming, or whatever. Being no dummy, she raised her hand, even though she'd never been saved. Remember, these kids learn to say "mine" before anything—bribing them with candy or games will only encourage lies and lip service.

It's Too Expensive

Establishing your own private school is going to cost you a lot, and maintaining it can be even more expensive over the long run. Most private religious schools offset these expenses by charging tuition. High tuition rates won't turn the kids into atheists, but might have that effect on their parents. Times are tough, and not everyone can afford expensive private school tuition with a free public school right down the street.

Scholarships are a handy way to keep kids in school, and can be supported by older, more financially secure devotees. Cult schools may want to devote a couple of hours of each school day to money-making chores. Consider setting up a call center, textile sweatshop, or brokerage house, and put those kids to work.

The Computer Lab Downloads Heresy

All those programs out there that supposedly protect your kids from the horrors of the Internet only go so far. Depending on what you find horrific, they might not provide any help at all. The more your kids are exposed to the outside world, the more likely they are to learn that not only is yours not the only religion in the world, but that others might be cooler. And once your kids realize you're uncool, it's all over.

Choosing Your Approach to Education

New religions likely won't have the funding necessary for that last category, the fully staffed and equipped full-day parochial school. But it's best to think about where you're headed early on, so that you can begin planning for the capital expenditure.

How did you answer the quiz in the Introduction when asked to complete the sentence: Children should be educated . . . ? This will give you some insight into how you should begin planning.

By Their Parents, in an All-vegan, Bully-free Home School Environment

Home schooling is gaining in popularity, aided by the Internet age, which can be a real help bringing otherwise expensive educational materials into your home. This is also a smart alternative for parents who are terrified of the outside world and hope to pass that crippling agoraphobia on to their children. The all-vegan thing is optional for cannibal cults, as is the bully-free environment for more assertive faiths such as the God of Aggressive Ignorance or the Cult of the Atomic Wedgie.

Cults, in general, favor home schooling, which keeps the kids on the compound and free from the threat of homosexual indoctrination, arrest on outstanding federal firearms warrants, the swine flu, and other dangers of the outside world.

A drawback to this approach is that when your religion's children eventually do wander out into the larger world, they will be entirely unprepared to deal with the people who say, "You believe *what*?" and burst into gales of laughter.

In Public Schools Where They Can Learn to Defend Their Faith Against Challenges

Most public schools scrupulously avoid anything that might indicate that they're forcing or even allowing kids to pray in a certain way to a certain god. Even traditions such as reciting the Pledge of Allegiance have come under fire, not for the weirdness of having children pledge their loyalty to a flag but for doing so "under God." In other words, public schools are not likely to endorse your religion's beliefs.

Still, sending your followers' children to public school can serve several useful purposes. First, it gives them the chance to serve as minievangelists. They can spread the word! (When you're working on your scripture, try to have at least some literature aimed at kids, to be handed out by kids.) Second, they can learn to defend their religion against challenges, such as science teachers. The resulting lawsuits might help you finally get the money together to establish a school of your own. Third, public school is free.

The drawback to this approach is that they may end up believing the science teacher instead of defending their faith against said science teacher. Some people temper this concern by not allowing their children into public school until they're adolescents and stop believing anything anyone says anyway.

In Private, Church-run Schools, Where They Can Be Successfully Indoctrinated

Most of the atheists I know are the product of a Catholic school education. For all intents and purposes, Catholic schools are atheist indoctrination camps. This is almost certainly not their intention. So, even though it may seem like a great idea to expose your followers' children only to your religion during school hours, before you set up an expensive private school that could blow up in your face, you'll want to consider why all those Catholic children grow up to be atheists. Reread the section "Avoiding Common Education Traps," earlier in this chapter.

In Public Schools Compelled to Teach Our Religion to All Kids

This is really taking it to the next level, inserting your religion into the public school curriculum. Even the incredibly big, really old, firmly established, and very well-funded major religions have mostly failed to do this in the United States, the occasional Christmas concert aside. But that doesn't mean you can't have this as one of your long-term goals.

Good luck.

In the School of Hard Knocks

Fundamentalist Mormon sects sometimes take the teenage boys from the compound, drive them to the nearest city, and drop them off. This is designed to cut down on the number of marriage-aged men in a polygamist society, but also tends to give these young men a real sink-or-swim education, a sort of outside world immersion program. The Amish do something like this, too. The basic idea is that once a young person gets a sense of how horrible the outside world is, compared to the tender embrace of the faithful, he's less likely to question the faith from then on.

Or, your religion might be based on a god who thinks kids are a pain in the ass and they should just take care of themselves. If they survive the mean streets long enough to find their way back to the compound, only then are they worthy to serve Crom!

Of course, the drawback to this approach is that none of the teenagers may come back, and they may spread the word about how cruel your religion is, thus putting a damper on recruitment and diminishing the number of followers you have.

Never

The ability to read and do math might not be all it's cracked up to be. Some of the most popular religions in the world were established in a day and age when very, very few people went to school, almost no one knew how to read, and the only history anyone ever learned was at church. If your religion demands that you maintain complete control over every aspect of your adherents' lives, you may not want anyone educated at all.

Also, school is, like, bogus.

The drawback to this approach is that you're surrounded by uneducated, highly religious people. Those kinds of folks have never done anything stupid, right?

CHAPTER 21

The Law of Man

*but only if you can't qualify
for tax-exempt status*

Unless you're starting one of those survivalist cults, and intend to entirely remove yourself and your followers from all outside influence, chances are your new religion is going to bump up against the government at some time. Generally speaking, state and federal government agencies actually do respect the constitutional separation of church and state and will not go out of their way to crack down on you, cast you out, blame you for all the missing pets in the neighborhood, and so on—so long as you actually aren't responsible for all the missing pets or committing other felonies such as running drugs or practicing human sacrifice (with or without cannibalism).

The Importance of Having Lawyers among the Faithful

Religious organizations are permitted to register as not-for-profit corporations, and can even avoid some taxes that for-profit businesses have to pay. Laws governing the status of religious organizations are written by lawyers to be read by lawyers so that people continue to need lawyers to read laws for them, sort of like religions used to do before the peasantry started learning to read. This being the case, as you're gathering your first round of converts, do your best to bring at least one lawyer into the fold. He or she can provide legal advice to you for free.

If your new religion practices divination, polygamy, or homosexuality; encourages listening to heavy metal or gangsta rap; or, in Syria, is anything but Islam, you may find yourself butting heads with the law, but for the most part it's taxes that you'll be concerned with. Along with that lawyer, try to convert an accountant, too.

The Tax-Free Myth

There's a common assumption out there that certain religious leaders are really only in it for the cash, and that cash comes to them tax-free. Though the former may be true, the latter is a little more complicated than you might think. It is true that churches (a government catch-all term covering any religious organization) can, and most often do, file with local, state, and federal authorities for tax-exempt status. That means a religious organization can ignore most, but not necessarily all, taxes on income it derives from donations and some other sources.

But people who work for the church and draw salaries, up to and including you, will still have to pay income tax just as you would from any other employer. The rules for what is and isn't tax-exempt are quite complicated and begin with the basic idea that a not-for-profit organization cannot be established in order to financially benefit an individual, including you. There are even rules about how much you can pay yourself in salary from the church coffers, based on salaries being paid by similar organizations in your area to people in similar jobs.

The specific rules vary from state to state and from year to year and go beyond the scope of this book. Seek professional help from an accountant at least, and maybe a lawyer. You can establish a not-for-profit corporation in most states fairly easily and with minimal fees, but tackling the IRS 501(c)(3) tax-exempt application is a daunting task, and comes with a filing fee of around $700. You don't have to file that right away, though, so you will have some time to pass the plate, hollowed-out skull, or whatever you're collecting donations in to raise that money.

Whoever wrote up IRS Form 1023, Application for Recognition of Exemption Under Section 501(c)(3) of the Internal Revenue Code, is obviously a member in good standing of the Scholars of the Particularly Long Book.

Government Intervention

The governmental body you're most likely to come in contact with first will be at the local level. The federal government is too big to suffer over every little evil death cult that might pop up here and there. If you fill out your 501(c)(3) paperwork properly and don't raise any red flags with the IRS or ATF, the feds are happy to let you be. States might rather you didn't do tarot card readings, but I have a feeling those laws are one halfway decent litigator in front of the Supreme Court away from going bye-bye. Let's hope the police and district attorneys in any state in the union have something better to do than demand you prove in a court of law that you're really seeing into the future.

But local governments, run by the weirdest of the weird, the busiest of the busybodies, and more often than not the most conservative of the conservatives in any given town, may not only notice that some kind of pantheistic temple devoted to deciphering the secret messages in the Cosmic Background Radiation of the Infinite Smooglameth is going up across from the Tastee Freeze, but will mostly likely throw themselves in front of it with all the gusto of a Saudi mutaween at a wet T-shirt contest.

Be prepared with a calm, legal response, and quote freely from the one holy scripture all U.S. citizens have in common: the First Amendment. As long as you keep the noise down and don't sue the city council for putting up a Christmas tree on the lawn in front of City Hall, eventually they'll move on to the gay couple who want to adopt a child, or worse, the black family that's looking at the old Wilson place.

CHAPTER 22

The Law of the Gods

cash, check, or major credit cards accepted

Every religion expects its followers to behave in certain ways and to follow certain religious laws. Long-established religions created these expectations hundreds or thousands of years ago, which can make some of them seem a little drastic in the contemporary world—like that whole thing about stoning your kids if they disobey you.

However, your religion is brand new, and that means you have an opportunity to think very carefully about what you'll expect of your followers and how that will mix with their day-to-day lives in our contemporary, technological society. So, for example, you can make it a law that every follower must start each day by sending out this standard tweet: "Join the Group of Really Hip People. Informational session every Weds. #justinbieber." Or, you can require them to add you to their cell phone plans, or whatever you think is an important religious law.

Basic Conduct During Worship

You will need to set some ground rules about how your followers should behave during worship services. This will ensure they bring the right attitude to the experience.

Posture

For example, what about the posture of your followers? Do you want people to bow, kneel, clasp their hands together, fold their arms in front of their chests, dance, stand, sit, and so on? Feel free to combine these movements so that your supplicants not only can offer up their requests, apologies, curses, and so on to the deities, but get a workout at the same time.

Chanting

It's an often-repeated truism that it's not what you say, but how you say it. Countless religions have used the chant as part of their rituals. Chanting resides in a space somewhere between speaking and singing. The rhythmic nature of it not only helps people remember the words but gives your services a great, old-school atmosphere.

Singing

Speaking of Justin Bieber, look at the power he holds over his adherents, and the legions of followers he's amassed—and he still isn't old enough to vote. Religions from all over the world use songs, or "hymns," to bring the congregation together in a common prayer. Creating hymns can be a real challenge if you aren't already a reasonably accomplished songwriter, but who says you have to do everything yourself? If you can convince an accountant in the flock to help you with your tax forms, surely you can find a songwriter out there among the penitents as well. It doesn't hurt to ask.

Cleanliness

How do you feel about dirty hands, or dirty feet? Do you want people to come before the gods as they would a job interview? Or would you rather they wallow around in mud first so that the deities see them as humbly having debased themselves, or that they're celebrating the Earth from which all life springs?

You might also consider how you want the inside of your temple to smell before locking this in.

Wardrobe

Demanding that your followers wear a robe or some other outfit will not only help them feel a part of a group but can be a nice side business to help fill the temple coffers. Most karate schools, for instance, make more money selling uniforms, belts, weapons, and whatnot than they do in class tuition. And having everybody dressed in the same red cowled robes will work toward knocking down your cultists' sense of individuality.

Thinking about Religious Laws

To start putting together your religious laws, you have to think about the general behavior you'd like to encourage in your followers. In the quiz in the Introduction, you were asked to at least start thinking about what your religion—your God/Goddess/Goat—expects from your followers. How did you answer?

Live a Life of Love, Peace, and Harmony with All His/Her/Their Creatures

It's hard to go wrong with this advice, but that answer contains some pretty broad categories. If you love all of your fellow creatures, which of them do you eat? More than one religion requires adherents to be vegetarians, or even vegans, but aren't carrots living things, too? What if someone tries to rob you? How do you live in love and peace with a guy who's in the process of punching you in the face? You will have to establish the answers to all of these questions, which may seem unnecessarily complicated. You could just leave it up to your followers' judgment, but then what do they need you for? If you choose this option, you will have to be prepared to spend a lot of time parsing hypothetical situations ("But what if the other person doesn't want to live in harmony with me?" "If I inadvertently hurt someone, is that as bad as intending to hurt him/her?" "If the end result is the same, why does my intention matter?") You may want to appoint an acolyte as the Answerer of Hypotheticals.

Seek Enlightenment

Sometimes religions begin when their founder achieves enlightenment. For instance, Ayya Vaikundar, founder of the Ayyavazhi faith, achieved enlightenment on March 3, 1833, and his sect was born. If you have not yet achieved a truly enlightened state yourself, you can still start your own religion, just base it on the ever-evolving and ongoing *search* for enlightenment. You don't even have to know precisely what enlightenment looks or feels like. When you get there, you'll know. You will want to make sure your followers don't get there before you do, so if they claim to have achieved enlightenment, you will need to define enlightenment as something other than what they've achieved.

Being Perfect Through Imperfection

Keeping the ultimate goal of your faith at arm's length can be a smart move. If you put yourself forward as an enlightened super-being, you're going to find that your followers develop very high expectations for you, carefully watching every tiny nuance of your speech and behavior for clues to their own enlightenment—or your insincerity. If you aren't ready to defend every misstep—every failed pass at an attractive petitioner, every secret burger run—make your own imperfection an example of how we're all on a journey together to someplace we hope we'll finally find, but it's really the *journey* that's the whole basis of your new religion.

The downside to this approach is that your followers will think you're just like they are, and so why are they tithing to you again?

Pray Regularly

Prayer can come in many forms and ranges from a few simple words of thanks to complex, lengthy rituals intended to get God/Goddess/Goat to take some specific action. Prayer is maybe the only thing besides that fundamental belief in a higher power that all religions have in common. You'll need to put long and careful thought into how you expect your followers to pray. Too much emphasis on prayer, however, can cause your followers to think what they say is more important than what they do. So instead of tithing to you they'll pray for forgiveness for not tithing to you. You can see the problems this could create.

Prayers

If you decide to include prayers in your religion, you'll want to offer your followers several options for speaking with God/Goddess/Goat. Remember that all prayers should start with an opening (e.g., "Dear Goat") to alert the deity in question that a prayer is in progress, and end with a closing ("Baaa!") to signal that the prayer is over.

- **Standard default prayer.** This is a simple prayer that even young children can memorize and that your followers can use in times of stress. If you don't have one of these—or if all of your prayers are lengthy and complex—then your followers might resort to using "Oh holy crap!" which is just undignified.
- **Standard situational prayers.** People don't want to think too hard, so you'll want to offer them some standard prayers to use in different situations. For example, you can have a prayer to say upon waking, one to say before or after eating, one to use after sex or maybe during sex, and so on.
- **Ritual prayer.** This should be a complicated procedure that includes special actions such as ritual hand positions, kneeling at certain inexplicable points, and so on. Ideally, only you and perhaps a few handpicked henchmen—that is, acolytes or deacons—will know how to lead the prayer, so your followers will have to come to services every now and then to fulfill their prayer obligations. Then you pass the hat.

Pay Regularly

Running a religion isn't cheap, and you're going to need your followers to kick in a little of the green stuff from time to time. I think you'll find there's a big difference in your asking for money and God/ Goddess/Goat asking for money. People might think you're just trying to profit from the faithful's quest for enlightenment, and you want to avoid that kind of suspicion among the devotees. Build into your scripture some form of tithing, and you can set your religion up with a nice, regular, more or less predictable income.

Tithes are generally 10 percent of each follower's income, or household income. You might want to specify in your scripture that's *before* taxes, too. Legally, tithes are voluntary, so though you may be able to excommunicate people who stop tithing, you can't sue them for the missing funds.

You will want to be careful not to appear too aggressive in the collection of tithes, unless you're running a death cult, because some people will leave your religion if you get too insistent, the ingrates. Don't be afraid to set up convenient payment plans, and to accept credit cards and PayPal. Also, you can always offer gift certificates for those hard-to-buy-for relatives. And don't forget to have an easily downloaded fill-in-the-blanks will form that followers can use to leave all their worldly belongings to you.

Rock

Who wouldn't want to worship a god who expects them to rock? But this might be a little hard to put your finger on, exactly. Think of it as a broad category including any nonspecific, hedonistic fun. The God/Goddess/Goat might expect you to dance 'neath the full moon's light. The Phallus of Infinity might want you to have sex at least once a week.

Keep in mind that cults based on chaotically wanton sex, drugs, and rock 'n' roll tend to burn out quickly. You're trying to *control* people's lives, not just watch them self-destruct. This is why the Phallus of Infinity only expects you to have sex once a week. Once a day is impractical for people with kids and jobs, or who are over the age of twenty-four, and though most people will be willing to try for it, be careful not to put your religion's requirements too far out of reach. Or, limit admission to your faith to those who pass a strenuous physical exam and who carry excellent health insurance.

Blow Up Stuff and Kill People in His/Her/Their Names

An awful lot of people have been killed in the name of one god or another over the long millennia of human history, so why should you all of a sudden have to be more enlightened? If you're creating a religion based on murder and/or terrorism, you'll want to secure a good criminal defense attorney up front, even before you sit down to write your scripture. Your lawyer can help with the language. For instance, if your holy book doesn't so much *require* violence as it does obliquely *avoid discouraging* it, you might have some defense at the inevitable trial.

The drawback to this approach? Ask Osama bin Laden or Charles Manson.

CHAPTER 23

Sample Religion 4: Sisterhood of the Perpetually Pregnant

birth control? we don't
even know what that is

The Sisterhood of the Perpetually Pregnant was founded in 1946 by Mrs. Gladys Ferguson of Parma, Ohio, nine months after her husband, Major Ronald Ferguson (U.S. Navy, Retired) returned from service in World War II. The Fergusons at that time began a fervent program of being fruitful, and being relatively young and in reasonable health, quickly multiplied. Then they multiplied again, and again, and again.

When Mr. Ferguson expressed his feelings, on February 3, 1951, that maybe four children was enough, Mrs. Ferguson filed for divorce and the Sisterhood of the Perpetually Pregnant was born.

The original sisterhood was a group of seventeen housewives, all from Parma, and all patients of the well-respected obstetrician Dr. Kimberly Gibbons. One of the first female practicing obstetricians in the state of Ohio, Dr. Gibbons, despite wild accusations in the press, was not a lesbian, but in fact a happily married mother of twelve herself. When she died tragically in a car accident, along with three of her twelve children, in 1960, Dr. Gibbons was canonized Saint Kim of the Hand-warmed Cervical Dilator.

In the late 1940s through the 1950s, the country experienced an unprecedented baby boom, and Mrs. Ferguson's first holy book, *What to Expect When You're Expecting Your Second Dozen Babies* was passed from woman to woman across the American Midwest via obstetrics nurses, midwives, and Avon Ladies, always well out of sight of any man.

The Sisterhood of the Perpetually Pregnant is one of the world's few truly matriarchal religions. Only women are invited to take the holy sacrament: a single prenatal vitamin every day. Only women are allowed into the most holy of sanctuaries, the Delivery Room. Only women, in fact, are allowed any rights under the Nine Monthly Laws of Grand Mother Gladys.

Had she taken the quiz at the beginning on this book, Grand Mother Gladys would have chosen "E. During the monthly Fornication Rite," for her answer to the question of when it's permitted to have sex. This rite is performed in the privacy of the woman's bedroom. Scripture describes certain sex positions in some detail, all designed to bring the seminal fluids closer to the egg in order to aid in conception. According to the Sisterhood of the Perpetually Pregnant, there is no reason to have sex except to procreate, so the sisters refrain from sexual contact except on the night of their greatest fertility.

If three months pass without a successful fertilization, the sister is required to find a new man. This doesn't have to be her husband (marriage is considered an entirely secular affair and is otherwise of no consequence) so long as the male is a fertile adult.

Men who have undergone vasectomies are known as "the Elderly," and are shunned by the sisterhood.

It is the goal of the members of the Sisterhood of the Perpetually Pregnant to have as many children as they can during their fertile years, and though few women manage it, all sisters are expected to have a baby every year. Any woman who has fewer than three babies in the first five years after her Insemination Ceremony is excommunicated.

Care of the resulting children falls to the entire sisterhood. It is considered unclean for a man to assist in any way, other than financially, in the upbringing of a child and it's become extremely rare for a sister to actually live with any of the men she uses to inseminate her.

The children of the sisterhood are sent to public schools, where they fly under the radar for the first eight years. Once in high school, the boys are sent off to military school and then into the world, as they cannot become full members of the sisterhood. The girls are instructed in the arts of achieving pregnancy and most are pregnant for the first time by the end of sophomore year.

In 1989 Janice Laurence, an attorney named Saint Janice when she died of complications after a cesarean section giving birth to her eighteenth child at the age of fifty-three, penned the greatest work of scripture since the founding of the religion. What has become known as Saint Janice's Waiver of Paternal Rights is an iron-clad agreement that effectively removes the father from not only any responsibility for the child he conceives with a member of the sisterhood, but any rights thereafter.

Before lying with a man for the Monthly Fornication Right, a sister is first required to don the Numinous Lingerie of Conception. This revealing but not-too-tight garment is sewn by her fellow sisters and given as a gift in something akin to a Secret Santa ceremony every Mother's Day (the Sisterhood of the Perpetually Pregnant's most holy of holy days).

She then presents herself to the man she's chosen to inseminate her. When he is suitably wooed, the sister excuses herself to the bathroom with the recitation of the Mother's Lie: "I'll be right back ... my diaphragm ..."

Once in the privacy of the bathroom the sister holds up her hands to the heavens and recites the following prayer:

In the warmth of the Goddess Womb

In the spray of the Wellspring of Life

In the tradition of Igbo

In the unpronounceability of Cihuacoatl

In the manner of Laima

In the shadow of Onuava

In the glory of Duggar

I offer up my womb to life once again

May the seed of [man's name] prosper in the belly of his woman

And may he then fuck off and let me raise the child in peace

Amen

Then they have unprotected sex.

Death: So You Can Make People More or Less Afraid

Next to clowns, death is the scariest thing anyone could possibly be confronted with. Avoiding it at all cost is so hardwired into our brains, people have committed graver sins trying to avoid death than trying to cause it. Despite millennia of mythology and séances, people know at the most primal level that death is not something you come back from, and people hate anything that's permanent. If your religion doesn't address death in a detailed way, your potential converts will go find a religion that does.

CHAPTER 24

Ashes to Ashes, Dust to Dust

*saying goodbye to
the dear departed*

Eventually, everyone buys the farm, bites the dust, settles in for the long dirt nap, shuffles off this mortal coil, or goes tits up. Any one or more of those things. Your religion, like literally every single other religion in all of human history, will have to address death. Fear of death is the reason people invented religion in the first place.

The subject of death-and-religion is vast, so let's get started. In this chapter, we'll focus on the funeral, and the events leading up to it.

Hello, Death

It doesn't always happen this way, but sometimes a person knows he or she is going to die—not eventually, but imminently. Either that or you know the guy lying on the floor here with some portion of his brain on the wall there is dying right now. Some religions have a solemn ceremony that allows the soon-to-be-departed an opportunity to get their journey to Elysium/the Howling Void/Thor's Great Hall in the Sky, etc.

off on the right foot. Having such a ceremony can be reassuring to your followers, so long as it doesn't include any clowns.

However, you may want to teach your followers to call 911 before they call you. If your adherents spend a few minutes trying not to die instead of, say, confessing their sins or making reservations for dinner with their favorite historical figures (personally, I would go with Albert Einstein, Julius Caesar, and John Belushi, in that order), they could possibly live longer and continue to tithe.

What about those followers with advance warning of death? You know the ones, they have oak wilt (particularly problematic among druids), an incurable form of cancer, or another disease that you know they're not going to recover from. If your religion features things such as suicide bombers, self-immolation, or voluntary human sacrifice, you'll want to have a ritual that prepares the participants in these rites for death, too.

Think about having the inevitably departed write a will or buy a life insurance policy, hopefully naming your church as sole beneficiary. Once that is accomplished, the follower will be eligible to receive your version of Last Rites. Here's a list of elements you may wish to include in your Good-bye [Insert Name Here] Ceremony:

- Take a cue from my favorite TV show and hold a ritual torch-snuffing ceremony in which the dying follower is asked to leave through the back door after hearing you say, "The gods have spoken."
- Very quickly weigh the person just before he dies, and then again right after. The difference is the weight of his soul. If there is no difference, he's faking it.

- Look the dying person in the eye and apologize for having lied to her when you told her she was going to Heaven. Y'know, just to screw with her.
- If the dying person is your celebrity spokesperson, have him tell you the name of two other celebrities he wants you to kill in his name. This is why celebrity deaths come in threes.
- Make sure to remind the soon-to-be-departed to go toward the light, or away from the light, depending on what your holy writings say about the light.

Preparing for the Funeral

Once your follower has died, and you have a dead body on your hands, you will need to do something with it. It is unlikely that the dead body will care, but your other followers will, and so, too, will the petty bureaucrats that are a blight upon an otherwise tolerable existence. For example, local health departments have strict laws about what you can and can't do with a dead body. Still, wave that First Amendment around long enough and you should be able to slip a pretty long list of funeral preparations past the bureaucrats. And I think you'll find most funeral homes are happy to work with you, for a substantial fee, on whatever you might require.

An Additional Precaution

If your religion fears vampirism, be sure to behead the body and place it between the deceased's knees so that if the body reanimates it won't be able to put its head back on. Lining the coffin with garlic and driving a wooden stake through the corpse's heart helps, too.

Before you start gathering your converts, and while you are still writing that massive epic poem, think about your religion's pre-funerary rites. You'll need to answer a few simple questions from the undertaker. For instance, do you want the body embalmed? Embalming preserves the body for a little bit—a few days at least, which allows the out-of-town relatives to gather for the funeral. But this does require a certain amount of messing about with the body. Maybe you want the still flesh of the faithful left untouched, unsullied by artificial chemicals. Okay, but then you better work into your Book of the Dead that funerals have to happen soon, or they'll turn into very unpleasant affairs—I mean, more so than a normal funeral. Other questions to consider include:

- Do you bury the body or cremate it? Or do you stick it on an ice floe, in a burning boat, or out on the prairie for the vultures to eat? Come up with a reason why. Perhaps the Great Scavenger in the Sky appreciates having its earthly counterparts taken care of, for example.

- Do you view the dead body before it's buried/cremated, and if so who is allowed to do the viewing? Again, explain why: To reassure everyone that the bastard is really dead? To force people to remember that life is ephemeral?

- Where is the body kept before it reaches its final disposition? Do you host your version of a wake, funeral, or memorial service at the temple, at the funeral home, at the deceased's home, or at the local recycling center?

- When and where do you implant the micro-RF tag so that when the Immortal Space Gods fly over in their UFOs they can find the body and bring it back to Zorkon for reanimation?

What to Bury/Burn/Destroy along with the Corpse

We'll talk about rising from the dead in Chapter 26, but in Victorian times, people used to rig up little bells that buried persons could ring if they woke to find they'd been buried alive by an undertaker who didn't really know how to feel for someone's pulse.

Like the ancient Egyptian pharaohs, you may require the death of all of the deceased's household servants, as well. Because most people don't have household servants anymore, you can sub in their smartphones, laptops, and maybe the occasional unlucky, if overly helpful, OnStar operator. Or, you can fashion little clay replicas and keep the booty yourself.

Things You Do at a Funeral

If marriage rites are the fun, happy, joyful celebration of life in your religion, funerals are the dour, depressing, futile recognition of mortality. But that doesn't mean they have to be all bad. Some religions have found ways to make funerals kind of a gas, like a big *bon voyage* party, happily sending the departed off to a better life in the Rolling Fields of Paradise & Casino. Depending on how awesome your afterlife is, funerals can be the high point of anyone's mortal life, like winning a trip to the Bahamas.

Even if your religion is less death-culty than that, you'll want to offer some solace for those left behind. We'll talk about the afterlife (if any) in the next chapter, but for now let's concentrate on what happens on the big day.

Funerary Rites

Here are some things you can add to your funerary rites. Feel free to mix and match as you see fit, and be creative. The only thing people love more than a good laugh is a good cry.

Pray

This is kind of a no-brainer, but take this opportunity to flip back to Chapter 22 and think about some kind of standard prayer to speak over a gravesite, while spreading ashes or while watching the vultures rip your grandmother's shriveled, naked corpse to bloody shreds. Funeral prayers serve two purposes: They make the living feel better about death, and they the draw attention of the gods to the incoming soul. I recommend a single prayer that does both, and that's easy enough for people to either remember or repeat back to you. Here's one, off the top of my head:

> O Zorkaz, who doth drive the Bus of Eternity
>
> Accept the Transfer of our faithful departed, [name of deceased]
>
> And convey her forthwith
>
> To the feet of Splurgal,
>
> the Lamb in the Center of the Infinite Who Judges with a Thousand Gavels
>
> And know that we who are left behind
>
> Are eventually going to get over it
>
> Amen

You know, or something like that.

Have a Party or a Parade

Who doesn't love the traditional New Orleans jazz funeral, in which a marching band plays a sad, minor-key dirge on the walk to the cemetery, and then a rousing Dixieland number on the way back, as if to say: "That's too bad Ol' Cletus's pushin' up daisies, but hell, we're all together, let's get *shitfaced!*"

Before you judge, you didn't know Cletus. That sumbitch weren't a-have it any other way!

Depending on where your temple is located, and how far away it is from the cemetery, permits for this sort of thing can be a hassle.

Feed the Wildlife

I wasn't kidding about that grandma-getting-eaten-by-vultures thing. People actually do that. If your temple is located anywhere but in some particular remote valley in, like, China or someplace, your converts might convert themselves out of your religion once they're forced to watch the first one of these "sky funerals."

Still, there is a trend toward so-called "eco-funerals," in which minimal preparation is done to the body, which is buried without a coffin, vault, or other container, somewhere out in the woods, and maybe you plant a tree over the deceased. Again, permits can be a bitch, and not everyone's going to have the stomach for it. They did it on an episode of *Six Feet Under,* and it was pretty gross.

Eulogies

This is the practice of taking turns getting up to a podium, pulpit, altar, or cenotaph and telling pithy anecdotes about the recently deceased in an effort to take the person down a notch so you don't feel so bad that he or she is dead.

A eulogy can be a liberating experience, full of laughter, tears, and closure, but inevitably some drunk second cousin who always had a bone to pick with that uppity bastard decides he deserves his say, or the matron aunt who will not shut up gets up there and does not shut up. Pulling her away from the microphone is just going to be sad, and really bring the whole thing down. And doing the same with the drunk guy is even worse. He will fight back, and probably puke.

If your holy writings include a list of people who are permitted to deliver eulogies, you can either avoid those scenes or encourage worse ones. Up to you.

Cry

Crying pretty much goes with the territory. Religions tend to assume it's going to happen and don't try to force the issue one way or the other. Rather than come down on either side of the issue, just make it a holy sacrament that if you do cry, you have to wipe your tears with the Holy Handkerchief of Fond Farewells, available at $12.99 a dozen at the temple gift shop.

Hey, Walt Disney made millions making people cry over dead parents, why can't you?

Spread Ashes in a Particular Place, Time, or Manner

A lot of people are opting for cremation these days. It's cheaper and faster, and if you do it before anyone starts raising questions along the lines of "come to think of it, Janet didn't go into anaphylactic shock when she was stung by that bee last year, so I wonder what *really* happened," you can avoid the whole autopsy problem . . . there are all sorts of good reasons to do it. Some people keep the ashes of the dear departed in an urn on the mantel or up on a shelf in the linen closet.

Some companies can even turn your said dear departed's ashes into diamonds, making them worth a lot more dead than they ever were alive—and who wouldn't love to sport Mom and Dad on her earlobes? But more and more people are asking that their ashes be spread in some particular spot. This could be anywhere that has some meaning to them (the river near where they grew up, the first mountain they ever climbed, the local liquor store), or might just be something like a nice hill overlooking the sea, or the sea itself, and so on.

You might want to consider making cremation not just an option but the only option for disposition of the body in your religion. This way you can have two funerals, one in which the congregation congregates to spread some of the ashes in a certain place significant to the individual who has died, and a second in which the rest of the ashes are spread in a certain (but different) place significant to the temple itself. This means you get to charge for the funeral twice, which can bring in as much as, say, twice the amount of money.

Sing

Hymns are prayers set to music, and they certainly have their place at funerals. Mozart's Requiem Mass is considered one of the greatest works of art in all human history. If you're looking for inspiration for a funeral hymn of your own, consider *Jeevan Maran Sukh Ho-e,* a Sikh funeral hymn by Guru Ram Das, translated from the original Gurmukhi:

She told us she was sick

She told us she was sick

Jeevan a-Mara-ran, she told she was sick

She really did look pale

She really did look pale

Jeevan a-Mara-ran, she really did look pale

Her husband's already dating

Her husband's already dating

Jeevan a-Mara-ran, the body's not even cold

I'm pretty sure that's the right translation, but not entirely. My Gurmukhi is a little rusty.

Warn People

In *Star Trek: The Next Generation,* when a Klingon warrior dies, the other Klingon warriors in attendance raise their voices in a raging howl, warning the gods that a Klingon warrior will soon arrive in Sto-Vo-Kor.

If your heavy metal death cult isn't doing this, you're a bunch of wannabe posers, unworthy of the blood spilled by your ancestors. And surely there will come a Great Retribution.

Don't say I didn't warn you.

Final Thoughts about Funeral Rites

As with other rites and ceremonies, funerals should be deeply rooted in your scripture and mythology. Are you running a cannibal cult? Well, serve up the dear departed quick before he starts to get gamey. Is death just a part of the "Circle of Life"? After the funeral invite everyone back to your place to watch *The Lion King*.

As it turns out, variety isn't just the spice of life.

CHAPTER 25

The Sweet Bye and Bye

what to expect when you're expecting an afterlife

Your religion doesn't have to recognize some kind of afterlife, but I'll caution you again about the whole religion-as-an-outgrowth-of-the-fear-of-death thing. Religions that promise an eternal afterlife in some kind of spiritual paradise have done very well, historically, and continue to attract the faithful, whereas those that propose the afterlife is a great howling void tend not to thrive.

Your religion should say something specific about what happens to us when we die—the more specific, the better. Because no one can report back with any accuracy what really happens after we die, you're free to let your imagination take flight.

Developing a Theory of the Afterlife

Your answer to the quiz in the Introduction will get you started on determining what happens during one's journey to the Great Beyond and, indeed, what the Great Beyond is. Look at how you finished the sentence, When you die, you . . .

Become One with the Universe or, Like, the Force or Something

What does it mean, exactly, to "become one with the universe"? That's the benefit to taking this approach: You're making a vague promise that leaves it up to your followers to fill in the blanks.

A lot of people, especially in the United States, live by some variation of the simple philosophy: Life sucks, then you die. Becoming one with the universe and living forever in a state of perfect peace adds a little hope: Life sucks, then you die, then nothing sucks.

Even I might be willing to tithe on the off-chance of that happening.

The downside to this approach is that many people want their afterlives to be more rewarding than sleep. These are the people who want streets paved with gold and seventy-two virgins, and, really, considering that they can't get their money back anyway, why not give them what they want?

Another drawback to this approach is that it's a little bit socialist for most Americans. We really don't like being one with anything. We like to be *number one* with everything. And there's a big difference.

Achieve Enlightenment on a Higher Plane of Existence

If this version of the afterlife could be captured in one truism, that truism would be "the grass is always greener on the other side of the fence." This afterlife appeals to those who are willing to accept that Earth is awful, but need something a little more specific waiting for them on the other side.

If you can promise enlightenment, and a better neighborhood, you'll win converts. The "higher plane of existence" is entirely up to you to describe. It's not precisely Heaven so much as it is a sort of personal playground, like a really cool resort hotel, wherein you live forever being smarter than anyone ever has been—you're so cosmically badass you don't even remember wallowing around in the mud with the lowly mortals of Earth. You have truly transcended.

What makes this afterlife so appealing for religious leaders is that it has a great built-in excuse for why no one can actually prove it's there. The former people who inhabit this lofty plane are so far above us it never even occurs to them to look back down and try to explain where they are and what they're doing to lower forms of life, i.e. humans. It would be like trying to describe mortgage-backed derivatives to your pet hamster.

On the other hand, not everybody is really all that keen on enlightenment. Some people think they already know everything there is to know, and would rather show up in the afterlife and be congratulated for being right all along.

Are Reincarnated Into the Body of a Human Baby

You know how you have your grandmother's eyes? Maybe that's not genetics after all. Maybe that's because she's you! The idea of reincarnation can be reassuring to believers and they will helpfully look for signs of it everywhere. All you have to do is give them a holy writ that describes the process in vague yet compelling detail.

This idea has some drawbacks, though. If new babies are born when someone dies, freeing up that soul to inhabit a new baby, how do you explain population growth? The human population has exploded in the past several decades—at a much higher rate than when most of the reincarnation-based religions were first created. You're going to need to make sure you add some kind of mechanism by which new souls are created, and whether or not it's better to be a New Soul or an Old Soul, and how you recognize that in yourself and others. Complicated, but fun.

Are Reincarnated Into an Animal or Something, but Hopefully Not a Bug—a Tiger or, Like, a Great White Shark Would Be Awesome

No judgment or anything, but this one never made sense to me. If I die and am reincarnated in the form of a panda, do I wake up and go, "Holy shit, I'm a panda!" or am I just reborn with the brain of a panda? In which case, what's the point of reusing me, a brilliant creative genius, if all I'm going to do for the next lifetime is sit in a zoo, scratch my ass, and not mate?

But savvy religious leaders could work the animal reincarnation angle to rationalize evolution. Say, your soul starts out as a bacterium, and with each lifetime you learn a little more—get a little smarter, more enlightened—until you finally make it to human. Then, savvy religious leaders could use the opposite as a threat: If you die and are reincarnated as a banana slug you're being punished for something. But you won't be a banana slug if you follow the rules of the religion. Brilliant, right?

The drawback to this approach is that there's always some asshole who actually wants to be a banana slug. It's become very popular to be a self-hating human, convinced that other animals are more pure or somehow more noble. Of course, not everyone feels that way and those who do will be cancelled out by the people who think humans are the chosen animal and everything else is just here for our amusement. Either way you go, you might be cutting out as many as half the potential converts in your community.

Go to Heaven/Next World/Arcadia If You've Led a Good Life, or Hell/Scary Bad Place/Underworld If You're a Sinner

For a while there, it seemed as though Hell was going out of style. It didn't really match up with the Oprah vision of God, did it? It was too old-fashioned, too mean-spirited. I masturbate a couple of times and it's third-degree burns for all eternity? That doesn't seem fair. Only recently has the fundamentalist movement brought Hell back, like Justin Timberlake brought sexy back. If you go the Heaven/Hell route, think very carefully about what might send one person to Hell and someone else to Heaven. You might want to give Hell a sliding scale, like a prison term. For masturbating a couple of times, God just burns you with a cigarette and then sends you up to Heaven, but if you kill somebody, settle in, sinner, you're going to be here for a while.

Or, you could have levels of Hell, as per Dante, with the outer levels a little farther away from the flames. Or, you could have various categories of not-Heavens, like Place Where One Is Forced to Watch *The Honeymooners* Endlessly or Nudist Resort Where Everyone Else Looks Like Margaret Thatcher or Barney Frank, and so on.

What If There's No Hell?

The Yazdani faith, practiced by fewer than a million people, mostly in Iraq, promises Paradise for the worthy, but sinners are consigned to oblivion—they are truly dead. There is no Hell. This is another popular version of the plane of punishment: It's not so much an orgy of torture and brutality as it is a place you're exiled to—the afterlife's cheap seats—far from the Grace of God.

In some cases, where you end up has something to do with how you died. This is true of certain Polynesian religions. And among the Bagobo, it's believed that each of us has two souls, one left (evil) and one right (good); a part of each of us goes to Hell and the other part to Heaven. This brings new meaning to the phrase, "Damned if you do, damned if you don't." Anyway, it takes a lot of the guesswork out of what happens after death.

Feel free to add your own twist to the terminology. Hell has come in many names and varieties: Gehenna, Hades, or Tartarus. Likewise Heaven could be Asgard, Olympus, or Nirvana. It's your multiverse, bring your own creative twist to it.

The plus to this approach is that people are already familiar with it, and therefore less resistant to it or inclined to question it. But at the same time, Heaven/Hell has a real been-there-done-that quality. And ultimately you're going to find yourself in a sticky situation when the weeping widow of a recently deceased follower is rendered inconsolable by the fact that she and her husband once had sex a week after the Monthly Fornication Rite, and now he's in the Screaming Citadel being sodomized by hate-daemons. What will she tell the children?

Rise Up as an Undead Avenger to Kick the Ass of All Who Wronged You in Life and Eat Their Livers in Front of Their Screaming Faces

The ancient Sumerians pretty much only had a Hell. Everybody went down to a terrible underworld to become a sort of ghost known as a Gidim, which then followed some living person around, kind of like a spirit guide.

The idea of coming back around for another try is something we'll get into in more detail in the next chapter. If your afterlife is more Earth-based, more about dead people haunting live people and less about the departed's existence on another plane of, er, existence, you may find that your followers would really like to be able to come back and kick their asshole bosses in the balls and visit other retribution upon those who are in dire need of it—without fear of getting into trouble. This is especially true of religions that incorporate motorcycles, Metallica, and/or blood into their rites.

However, this approach can seem a little, well, violent and aggressive to many people, especially those who suspect they would be getting kicked in the balls by angry ghosts.

Keep in mind that a religion that asserts that dead people come back to hang out with the living doesn't mean that the haunting/return to Earth/transition to another state of being has to all be off a Megadeth album. You could come back to help, guide, and protect people just as easily as you might come back to exact your bloody revenge, or drop your mortal enemies' toothbrushes in their toilets just to mess with them.

CHAPTER 26

Back and Better than Ever

rebirth and ascension,
not necessarily in that order

Anything can happen in your new religion. You are the master of time and space, life and death, good and evil. So why end with a funeral, and consign the eternal spirits (if any) of your departed followers to eternity when you can bring at least some of them back for another go at it?

How, when, and why your dead disciples might return to the world of the living is limited only by your imagination . . . or, I mean, *revelation*.

What the Dead Do after Death

Trying to figure out what the dead do after death can be a bit of a challenge. To help sort it out, take a look at your answers to the quiz in the Introduction. The question was: After death, the truly holy will . . .

The potential answers were:

Get a Second Chance to Lead a Better Life

In the previous chapter, we talked a bit about reincarnation. This is the idea that after you die, your soul comes back to the world of the living in a different physical form. The concept of a soul is common to most religions, and comes with many names. You can call this an eternal spirit, qi, life force, or make up a whole new word for it, maybe with roots that make it sound like a "real" word. How about "essenceverence," or "eternality"?

If your polytheistic religion includes a god of death (or a god of rebirth) you might want to tie the intangible life force to that deity, giving him/her/it jurisdiction over what the dead follower comes back as, and so on.

The Endless Cycle

Several Eastern faiths, including Buddhism, Hinduism, and Jainism, embrace the idea of an endless cycle of birth, death, and rebirth. The philosopher Arthur Schopenhauer wrote about the idea of a nonlinear timeline and proposed that when we die, we are reborn not as someone else or as a sea cucumber but as ourselves, to live our lives over again, and keep doing so over and over and over again, maybe with the hope that eventually we'll get it right and achieve some kind of higher state. I tend to agree with the philosopher Woody Allen, who commented on this subject: "Great, that means I'm going to have to sit through the Ice Capades again. It's not worth it."

Sometimes the second chance at life comes almost instantaneously. People have been "pronounced dead" and a few minutes later resuscitated, returning to the world of the living after having gotten just enough of a glimpse of the Great Beyond to offer advice and sell books to the living.

If you want your religion to embrace the so-called "near-death experience," make sure your holy epic poem/monthly catalog contains very detailed descriptions of what people can expect to see in the first few seconds after death, then be sure to repeat this as often as possible—really hammer it home. Then, when one of your followers is hanging at the edge of death after a traumatic accident, her fevered imagination will naturally go there and *voilà*, your afterlife has now become real.

The downside of this, though, is that you may not have a chance to suitably brainwa—I mean, *enlighten* your flock before one of them almost dies. Whatever story that follower brings back from the other side could really screw you up, even if she comes back with no story at all.

Guide Loved Ones from the Great Beyond

You don't have to physically reconstitute—into your own body, a new body, or a chipmunk's body—in order to effectively return from the dead. Your religion may allow for the ever-popular incorporeal spirit guide.

Spirit guides, like any supernatural being, can come in any form your unique revelation might lead you to describe. If you do a little research into spiritualism you'll get all sorts of interesting ideas for rites and ceremonies that involve contacting the disembodied spirits of the deceased. Once called from the afterlife by a medium, or one of your priests, or yourself, or any of your followers, the spirit is then asked a series of questions starting with simple stuff like, "Grandma? Is that you?" all the way up to, "If I fail to report to the unemployment office the $37.23 I made from my garage sale, will I end up being arrested for fraud?"

You might want to think of a more philosophical question than that, but you get the idea. Because spirits tend to be loath to just pull up a chair and start talking, you may want to tweak your séance rituals to only allow for yes or no questions, so the spirit can just knock on the table once for yes, twice for no. Charlatan mediums can then provide the answers themselves by surreptitiously knocking on the bottom of the table. Your religion is *real*, though, so you won't need to do anything like that.

In order to prevent your followers from depending more on their dead grandparents for advice than they depend on you, you might want to limit the number of people who are able to break through the eternal boundary between life and death. This could also serve as a potential reward for the most faithful of your congregation. Catholic saints pretty much fall into this category, but they're usually entities you pray to for help in a specific situation rather than conjure in a séance. Still, it might be useful to appropriate the word "saint," but then add the séance twist to it. The possibility of becoming a saint after death gives your followers something to strive for.

You should also consider the concept of the dream visitor. When people suffer a death in the family, it's not uncommon for those people to dream about the recently deceased. If, in your holy writing, you make it clear that this is not simply a dream, it's the recently deceased trying to communicate with the bereaved via their dreams, I think you'll find little resistance to this idea among your cultists. It's one of the few things in the spiritual world you can predict with any accuracy, which will really help bolster your attempts to come across as the person with all the answers.

This sort of subpantheon can give your religion some fun variety, but can also make the whole thing too complicated. The longer your religion is around, the more of these creatures you'll accumulate, until you end up with the Patron Saint of Garlic Sausages.

A Word about Contact with the Dead

People are drawn to the idea of an afterlife for two reasons. First, everyone wants to think that there's something more to life, that it isn't just as short and meaningless as it would otherwise seem. And second, people hate the idea of their loved ones disappearing into oblivion, never to be seen or heard from again. Proposing that dead people come back to act as spirit guides for those who are alive covers both bases, which will be quite a draw for your religion. The difficult part is managing your followers' expectations. Don't over-promise in terms of what they can expect to see, hear, and feel from the dead. Nothing drives converts away faster than unfulfilled promises. But don't be afraid to find ways to help them get what they want, with you as the conduit of all contact. Maybe you're the only one who can speak to the dead, and perhaps you can only do it on alternative Wednesdays once you're adequately liquored up. Or it's possible that our spirit guides leave signs all around us, but only you and perhaps a select few acolytes who have undergone rigorous and expensive training can interpret them. You can warn your followers that trying to interpret the signs themselves is potentially problematic, but for a small contribution to the roof fund, you'd be happy to do a professional reading.

Become an Angel

Feel free to borrow the idea of angels, just as you did saints, but change the name to give it a new twist of your own. Spirit beings that function as guides, avengers, messengers, and guardians (and demons, too, for that matter) are found in many religions, and are particularly popular in polytheistic and pantheistic faiths.

Sometimes these guides are people who've died and were rewarded with transformation into some powerful new servant of the gods. This kind of thing can end up giving your religion a competitive flavor that not everyone will be drawn to. Some people will know that although they're pretty much loyal followers, their tithe from working at Wendy's is never going to compete with the tithe from the hedge fund manager, so you tell me: Which one's going to end up becoming an angel?

Of course, if the hedge fund manager is happy enough, you can probably stand to lose the fry cook.

Let's take a closer look at seven broad categories of servitor being that your deceased followers might transform into after death. Each category has a good guy (angel) and a bad guy (demon) version. Sometimes, it's hard to tell which is which.

Defenders

Sometimes the gods get worried about people and find it necessary to lend a hand. If your religion includes defender angels—supernatural bodyguards protecting the lives or goals of the most devout—be prepared to answer some of those difficult questions we've addressed at various points in this book. Why didn't one of these defender angels show up on at least one of the flights hijacked on 9/11? And if anything bad happens to someone who regularly attends your temple rites, keeps up with her tithing, and sleeps with you on command . . . well, where the hell was Rahim the Holy Linebacker when she needed him?

Warriors

The gods occasionally call on people to march off to *jihad*, but human foot soldiers are only effective against human heretics. When the gods start to fight each other, they may send their mortal followers to fight it out on Earth, but what about Homeland Defense? Warrior angels and demons fight other warrior angels and demons in the really big, really important battles between Heaven and Hell, or between the Realm of Sleep and the House of Alarm Clocks, and so on.

If you have a mortal follower who's been really good about fighting the heretics on the ground, promise him a position as a warrior angel in the afterlife.

Heralds

The gods don't like to show up unannounced. I think they're worried it'll freak people out too much. So they often send representatives from the spirit world (or Olympus, or whatever) to speak with humans on their behalf. A herald is someone who rides out ahead and says something like, "Get ready, everybody, the boss is on his way." But they could also warn of other things, like impending disasters, or that your 401(k) is about to take a huge hit if you stay so heavily in tech.

Ferrymen

I'm not sure precisely why, but mythology is silly with ferrymen. They're everywhere, ferrying people across this or that, on their way from here to there, and various funeral practices have been created to appease them, such as burying people with money to pay the ferrymen. Folk-rock singer-songwriter Cat Stevens (before his conversion to Islam) advised bringing tea for the tillerman.

Think of the ferryman as a broad category of angel or demon that handles transitions, especially the transition from life to death, Purgatory to Heaven, and so on. Look for places in your scripture where people or their life forces go from here to there, and assign a ferryman to help. It's an important job, and maybe the ferryman is replaced from time to time. Helpful people among your followers, such as Hospice nurses or midwives, can become ferrymen when they die.

Torturers

If you don't think angels torture people you haven't read the Old Testament lately, but most people consider this the responsibility of demons. Your evil death cultists will love believing that if they're really super-badass in life, they won't go to Hell to be tortured for all eternity, but will *get to* torture others for all eternity. This could keep the most aggressively sociopathic amongst your devotees happy—and they need to be kept happy.

Tempters

How do you know if your followers are really devoted to your religion, are absolutely committed to doing the right thing (as you see it)? You might want to try to tempt them away from the fold and see how quickly they turn on you. Almost anything you don't want people to do can be blamed on the efforts of a tempter angel (or demon).

Does your religion strictly ban the use of drugs? If so, the guy on the corner slinging crack isn't just somebody who's made a poor career decision, but a manifestation of the demon Crackolius. The tempter spirit is a powerful mind-control . . . I mean, *inspirational* tool, and is especially effective against the people in your coven who don't really want to do crack anyway.

Become a Ghost

Religion, mythology, folklore, and television are so chock-full of different kinds of ghosts and undead creatures it can be a little overwhelming trying to figure out how your religion should come down on the subject. Most of the time, ghosts and undead beings such as ghouls and vampires are considered a bad thing, but of course that isn't true for your vampire blood cult.

Ghosts tend to be the disembodied spirits of people who don't realize they're dead, or don't want to be dead. If your religion thinks this is a bad thing, that means you tend to see the afterlife as a good place someone shouldn't want to avoid. If death truly is an end of all things, total oblivion, then who would blame people for wanting to come back, even if it's just to wander around in attics rattling chains and rearranging people's medicine cabinets?

I think you'll find that most people are ready to believe in ghosts, and are just as likely to believe you if you tell them ghosts are bad as they are to believe that ghosts are good. If you spend too much time emphasizing ghosts, though, your religion might end up seeming a little spooky, for want of a better word. Of course, if you swap out the word "ghost" for "spirit," "phantasm," "apparition," or "incorporeal soul-remnant," you could get a little more mileage out of it.

Become a Demigod

Demigods are divine beings that, for various reasons, are not quite fully at the level of gods. Demigods generally don't have mortal worshipers, or temples organized in their names, but they're a step above the angels and demons, and other servitor beings. Demigods have more independent will and personality, too, and some of the most popular classical myths are about demigods, such as Hercules. Your really super-devout followers might qualify for demigod status after they die.

Demigods are often the heroes of the pantheon. If your religion has warrior demons and/or angels, who leads them? The heroic demigods are the generals of the divine host. Sometimes, like Hercules, they act more independently, as superhero versions of defenders, tempters, and so on.

The term "demigod" has sometimes been used to describe the off-spring of a god and a human. This is another popular motif that's been used and reused since the dim recesses of ancient times. You might want to put yourself forward as the son or daughter of a god (or the God) and a mortal woman, or a goddess (or the Goddess) and a mortal man—or whatever. Maybe your religion allows for same-sex divine insemination.

Sometimes, though, this genetic link to God is only clarified after the demigod in the making first shuffles off his or her mortal coil, then arises as the heir apparent to God.

If you want to put yourself forward as a demigod people will expect to see you do something demi-miraculous. Hercules was capable of incredible feats of strength. What are you really good at? If you're a C.P.A., you might be the son of a mortal woman and Excel, the Keeper of the Holy Ledgers. If you've got a talent for basketball, you're obviously one of the myriad Bastards of Saint Wilt.

That last one has a high probability of actually being true.

But then you have to be really good at those things, and I mean Olympic-level good at it, or someone's going to doubt you. And once one person doubts you, that doubt can spread like a virus.

Become a New, Way More Badass God

How many gods are there in your polytheistic pantheon? Is there room for one more?

The right to ascend to godhood is something you'll want to reserve for only your most super, over-the-top, ridiculously, especially most devout of the devout. Or, reserve it for yourself.

Here on Earth you may be merely the mortal High Priest Emeritus (or Chairman of the Board for purposes of your 501(c)(3) paperwork), but when you die, like Obi-wan Kenobi, you will become more powerful than (whoever it is you're warning of this) can possibly imagine.

Any time you add a new deity to the pantheon, you have to pay careful attention to balance. Think of it as a corporation. Most companies don't just hire people willy-nilly and let them figure out what they should do. If your company needs a payroll administrator, you hire a payroll administrator. Likewise, if you've sensed a need, since your last draft of the holy scripture, for a Lawyer God, then put that bug in the ear of the lawyers in your congregation. Make it clear that the one who does the most *pro bono* work for you, or who settles the most high-price separation of church and state lawsuit on your behalf, will achieve this divine position when he or she dies.

Godhood can also depend on intangibles. Not every pantheon is profession- or specialty-based. You might not have a God of Logistics or a Fertility Goddess, but will have gods and goddesses of things such as love, hope, anger, or the color orange. The trick is to identify something in the demeanor, or hobbies, and so on, of your super-follower and sometime after the funeral, announce to the gathered coven that Sister Florence has ascended to the godhead and is now Florence of the Pretty Smile, or She Who Really Lights Up When She Sees a Puppy.

Consider, too, whether you want your followers to believe that you actually already have died and returned. You don't necessarily have to prove this—religion is about faith, not fact—but put some effort into a convincing story, anyway. Promise demigodhood to a few people who'll be willing to corroborate your story of having died when you fell off the balcony at that frat party, and coming back to life three days later in that one chick's dorm room.

Yeah, man, he was totally, like, dead, and shit. I saw it.

People like rewards. They like to have something to strive for. Promising godhood to the most worthy will make at least some of your followers work very hard to set themselves apart from the rest of the flock. But again, the downside is that there will be some people among your congregation who know they're not up to the task, and might end up getting bitter and resentful.

CHAPTER 27

Sample Religion 5:
The Holy Undertakers of Giltiné

additional funeral parking in rear

Once relegated to obscure Lithuanian folklore, since the fall of the Iron Curtain worship of this terrifying death goddess has gained new popularity. In 1991, Daiva Vydûnas, the bastard daughter of Lithuanian writer Vilius Storostas-Vydûnas, founded the Holy Undertakers of Giltiné after reading a recently declassified *New Yorker* article about nondenominational churches in the southern United States. Eager to enter the brave new world of post-Soviet capitalism, many budding Eastern European entrepreneurs flailed about in a like manner, but Daiva hit a gold mine with her unique spiritual business plan.

First, she widely publicized the ancient folklore of Giltiné, telling and retelling the grim tales of this goddess of death with a style and aplomb that almost made people believe she was the daughter of a famous author. This familial connection was never adequately proven, though, and supposedly there was a cease-and-desist letter written, and suddenly Daiva Vydûnas became known simply as Lady Daiva.

Regardless, her holy writings are scary stuff.

213

Giltiné appears variably in the form of a venomous snake, an owl, or a gaunt, pale woman dressed in flowing white robes. She is the sister of the co-death goddess Laima, but whereas Laima has a soft side, comforting the dying to ease their transition into the next world, Giltiné actually kills people. It's a bit more of a direct approach, but rather more efficient.

Traditionally, Giltiné administers a deadly kiss, passing on her enervating venom, but Lady Daiva's twist on the legend has come to include various manifestations of Giltiné's murderous powers. Now, she causes car accidents, strokes, various forms of cancer, and the occasional tsunami.

In an effort to dodge an ongoing Interpol investigation, Lady Daiva's holy writings have begun to make it clear that only Giltiné herself is authorized to actually take a human life. Her mortal worshipers are free to pray to their goddess to draw her attention to someone they think should die, but are not allowed to kill someone themselves.

Temples of the Holy Undertakers of Giltiné operate in thousands of locations under the secular name Amalgamated Funeral Services, Inc. Lady Daiva has identified two different groups of followers, alternately referred to as the Willing and the Unwilling, or the Undertakers and the Customers.

Funeral rites range wildly, given that it's the act of killing that the Holy Undertakers of Giltiné worship. Followers are expected to study the funeral practices of other religions, and are encouraged to develop a deep respect for the entire spectrum of rites and ceremonies. The Holy Undertakers of Giltiné don't impose funeral practices, they facilitate them. When an Unwilling/Customer rates a Holy Undertaker all five out of five on the Sacred Satisfaction Survey, this is recorded in the Permanent Record of the temple. Once a month, the congregation of the Willing/Undertakers gather to congratulate the devout recipient of the most five out of fives as Holy Undertaker of the Month.

The various forms of the afterlife are equally respected by the Holy Undertakers of Giltiné. The Undertakers work toward a state of eternal servitude in which they're occasionally granted the opportunity, by the Most Hideous Goddess Herself, to actually cause the death of a mortal. After all, when you work around the effect all day, you eventually feel the urge to try the cause on for size.

But for the most part, Giltiné is an ambivalent mistress who goes about her work without a thought to her mortal followers, who honor her by cleaning up after her.

Particularly devout Undertakers (those who achieve steady 20 percent profit margins and 10 percent year-over-year gross revenue growth) are deemed Most Valuable Undertakers, and are in line (based on temple-wide annual profit reviews) to ascend to the state of Vice President in Charge of Death. These glorious angels follow behind the sisters Giltiné and Laima, doing the sweeping up and getting coffee—whatever the holy sisters need—for all eternity.

It is the highest sacrilege to assert that someone could return from the cold embrace of death. After all, that would mean that Giltiné failed in her efforts to send the expired soul on to its Great Reward . . . whatever that is. When confronted with tales of ghosts or the undead, the Holy Undertakers of Giltiné strenuously debunk even the most obviously fictional account.

They take the whole death thing really, really seriously.

So You've Started Your Own Religion

*go with the gods, my friends,
but be careful out there*

So you've started your own religion—good for you! Now you're going to be confronted with all of the stuff that's not in this book. It's a slim little volume, and we're talking about a huge subject that has occupied the majority of the human race for as long as there has been a human race, so cut me some slack already.

But no matter what life as a cult leader, holy person, Grand Vizier, or Spiritual Janitor may bring you, at least you're getting up off your dead ass and doing something constructive with your life. Think about all those people who don't start their own religions, but sit around complaining about people who have.

Now they get to complain about you, too.

Starting your own religion can have enormous benefits for you spiritually, financially, and emotionally. If you're the center of a center of worship, you get loads of attention, and who doesn't love being the center of attention? Hell, you could even get your own reality show someday. Although all this may have come across as cynical from time to time, maybe you actually will achieve some spiritual enlightenment. I hope so. And if you play your cards right, you can come out with a sweet little nest egg to boot.

Of course, there are downsides to everything, and starting your own religion will present you with all sorts of challenges on your road to universal harmony and/or mastery. Competition for the spirits/souls/life essences of the masses is stiff, and you'll come up against some heavily entrenched opponents who don't like the idea of a whole new credo suddenly popping up across the street, across town, or even across the country. You'll have to manage your own fanatics and other peoples', and fend off all sorts of wild tales about human sacrifice and liberal voting bias, even if you're not actually doing either of those things.

But chin up, the odds are actually in your favor. The world seems like a pretty grim place right now. The economy sucks, politics is off the rails, and a lot of unemployed people have extra time on their hands. These conditions are ripe for the establishment of all sorts of new faiths that can help people feel better about their crappy lives. If you don't fill that gap for them, someone else will.

So go out there and preach it, brothers and sisters.

Preach it well!

INDEX

Adulthood rites, 18, 119–23
Afterlife, 21, 193–99, 201–12
Ahl-i Haqq, 138
Algonquins, 120
Ali, Muhammad, 82
Anahita, 114–15
Angels, 205–08
Animal sacrifice, 141–42
Atheism, 26, 162
Ayyavazhi faith, 172

Bad things, reasons for, 34
Baldwin, Stephen, 85
Beatles' albums, 40
Benefit concerts, 109
Billboards, 78
Blood rituals, 48
Books, 38–39
Brochures, 76–77
Buddhism, 82, 114
Buildings, 104–06

Calendar, 15, 51–56
Cathedrals, 104–05
Catholic Church, 59, 113–14
Celebrity spokesperson, 16, 75, 81–86
Ceremonies, 17. *See also* Rituals
Chanting, 170
Children, 20, 119–23
Chinese Capping Ceremony, 121
Christianity, 26

Church, physical place for, 101–09
Church of Phil, 95–98
Cleanliness, 171
Con artists, 7–8
Contentment, 72–73
Converts, 69, 71–79
Court of Lazarus, 48
Cow jumping, 120
Creation story, 34
Cremation, 186, 190–91
Cruise, Tom, 81, 84–85
Crusades, 91, 94
Cult of the Blue Öyster, 145–47

Day of Anahita, 114–15
Death, 21, 181, 183–92
Defenders, 204
Deity(ies), 13, 20, 25–31
Demigods, 209–10
Demon Revels Da Meur, 116–17
Discipline, 133–34
Divorce, 154
Dogma, 23
Donations, 135–36, 141, 174–75
Doomsday cults, 53
Dream visitors, 204
Drinking rituals, 131–32

Earth-centric religion, 54
E-books, 39
Eco-funerals, 189

Education, 20, 157–63
Enlightenment, 71–72, 172–73, 194–95
Entrails, 40–41
Epic poem, 36–37
Eternal life, 72. *See also* Afterlife
Ethics, 34
Eulogies, 189–90
Excommunication, 19, 133–38
Extortion, 108

Faithless, expulsion of, 19, 133–38
Fanatics, 16, 87–90
Feast of St. Wando, 113–14
Feasts, ritual, 46–48
Ferrymen, 205
Festa das Mocas Novas, 120–21
Flyers, 76
Followers, acquiring, 71–79
Food rituals, 44–48
Fundraising, 106–09
Funeral rites, 21, 184–92

Gay marriage, 126
Gere, Richard, 82
Ghosts, 198–99, 208–09
Gibson, Mel, 84
God(s), 13, 20, 25–31
    accession to, 210–12
    dead, 31
    nature of, 29–31
    number of, 29
Good things, reasons for, 34
Government, 20, 165–68
Graduation ceremony, 122
Gregorian calendar, 52, 54
Guinn, Marian, 137

Hallucinogens, 49, 120
Hamar, 120
Heaven, 196–98
Hell, 196–98
Heralds, 205
Heretics, 57–62, 134–38
Hinduism, 112–13, 122
Holy days, 17, 111–17
Holy rites, 15, 17, 43–49. *See also* Rituals
Holy texts, 33–41
Holy Undertakers of Giltiné, 213–15
Holy wars, 17, 91–94
Home-based church, 102–03
Home schooling, 160–61
House of worship, 101–09
Hubbard, L. Ron, 63
Human sacrifice, 142–43
Hymns, 191–92

Illegal drugs, 49
Imbolc, 113
Infidels, 91
Inquisition, 15, 57–62
Internet, 79, 160
Islam, 82

Lakewood Church, 104–05
Legal issues, 165–68
Life instructions, 149
Love, God as, 29–30
Lovecraft, H.P., 9

Madonna, 85
Maher, Bill, 83
Makar Sankranti, 112–13
Mardudjara aborigines, 122–23
Marriage, 18, 125–32, 151, 153–54

Martyrdom of the Bab, 115
Mass media, 78
Mega-church, 104–05
Metempsychosis, 138
Miracles, 55–56
Money, 141, 174–75
Monotheism, 26–27
Mormons, 163
Mortal sins, 135

Nation of Islam, 82
Near-death experiences, 202–03
New Religious Movements, 8
Nouruz, 113

Objects, burning/burying, 140–41
Oprah, 81
Oral tradition, 35–36
Orgies, 154–55
Origin story, 34

Pamphlets, 76–77
Pancake breakfasts, 107
Pantheism, 26–28
Pantheon, 27–29
Paranormal phenomena, 8
Parochial schools, 157–60, 162
Penance, 133–34
Philip Experiment, 8
Philmas, 116
Philosophy, 26
Polygamy, 126, 127
Polytheism, 26, 27, 28
Pope, 59
Prayer, 134, 173–74, 188
Promotional strategies, 76–79
Public schools, 161–62

Public spaces, 103–04
Publishing, 39

Quecholli, 116

Radio, 78
Ramadan, 121–22
Reincarnation, 138, 195–96, 201–02
Religion
    acquiring followers for, 71–79
    ease of creating, 9
    promotional strategies for, 76–79
    questions to ask before starting,
        12–22
    steps to creating, 11–12
Religious laws, 169–76
Religious leaders, types of, 7
Religious principles, 14
Religious texts, 13, 33–41
Rental spaces, 103–04
Revenge, 73
Rings, 132
Rites of passage, 18, 119–23
Rituals, 99
    adulthood, 119–23
    funeral, 184–92
    holy rites, 15, 17, 43–49
    marriage, 125–32
    place to perform, 101–09
    sacrifices, 19, 129, 139–44
    sexual, 154–55
Rules, 35, 149, 169–76

Sacraments, 136–37
Sacred rites, 15, 17, 43–49
Sacrifice, 19, 129, 139–44
Same-sex marriage, 126

Samhain, 116
Satanists, 143
Scholars of the Particularly Long Book (SPLB), 63–67
Schools, 157–63
Scientology, 85
Sex, 19, 73–74, 136, 151–55
Shakers, 7
Sheen, Charlie, 85–86
Shotgun weddings, 131
Signs, 77
Singing, 170
Sins, 135, 138
Sisterhood of the Perpetually Pregnant, 177–80
Social media, 79
Soul, 201–02
Spanish Inquisition, 59–62
Spirit guides, 203–05

Taxation, 165–67
Tea rituals, 45–46
Television, 78
Temples, 104, 106
Tempters, 208
Ten Commandments, 38
Terrorism, 175–76
Tithe, 135–36, 174–75
Torturers, 208
True believers, 7
Tukuna, 120–21
Twinkies, 108–09, 128

Uncaring God, 30
Unity symbols, 132
Urban II, 91

Vans, 77
Vesak, 114
Violence, 175–76
Virgin sacrifice, 143–44
Vows, marriage, 129–30
Vulcanalia, 115

Wardrobe, 171
Warriors, 204–05
Websites, 79
Wedding attire, 130–31
Wedding gifts, 128–29
Weddings, 125–32
Worship services, 170–71
Wrath of God, 31
Wristbands, 107

Yazdani faith, 197
Year One, 55
Year Zero, 54

Zoroastrianism, 113

About the Author

Philip Athans is a bestselling fantasy author who has invented his share of religions for the strange alien worlds he's inhabited his entire life. This has given him a keen appreciation for the difference between fantasy and reality, which he hopes the rest of the world will one day share.

DAILY BENDER

Want Some More?

Hit up our humor blog, The Daily Bender, to get your fill of all things funny—be it subversive, odd, offbeat, or just plain mean. The Bender editors are there to get you through the day and on your way to happy hour. Whether we're linking to the latest video that made us laugh or calling out (or bullshit on) whatever's happening, we've got what you need for a good laugh.

If you like our book, you'll love our blog. (And if you hated it, "man up" and tell us why.) Visit The Daily Bender for a shot of humor that'll serve you until the bartender can.

Sign up for our newsletter at

www.adamsmedia.com/blog/humor

and download our Top Ten Maxims No Man Should Live Without.